Hiring For Sales:

The Essential Guide to Navigating the Sales Talent Acquisition Process

CHRISTOPHER GOFF

A Starting Simple Series

Hiring For Sales: The Essential Guide
to Navigating the Sales Talent Acquisition Process

PAPERBACK ISBN:

979-8-9862249-8-5

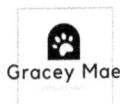

Gracey Mae

Read the Newsletter

The Sales Comp Guy Newsletter is a bi-weekly email all about managing sales, from compensation plans, to scaling your salesforce, to company culture, and beyond.

Each email brings you information on topics like:

- The importance of being a culture-first company when hiring for sales

- Navigating the challenges of employee retention in the current labor market

- Tips for sales and performance management

- Steps for managing the financial viability of your sales compensation program

- The ins and outs of compensation plan mechanics

We also link you to other resources for staying up to date on sales force management. And we welcome any questions or requests for content.

Sign Up Today

Or Scan the Code to Sign Up

Praise for the Starting Simple Series
Finding Fairness

Christopher Goff offers up a Zen-like approach to addressing the very important topics of fairness, equity and transparency in designing sales compensation programs. Philosophically, he is spot-on; but, most importantly, Christopher gives the business professional all of the necessary pragmatic structure and details (enhanced with real-life stories and scenarios) to ensure the successful design and administration of reward programs that will inspire and motivate the sales workforce. Truly a must-read - without question, you will gain value from this book!"

– JOHN R.

Chris walks the reader through all of the areas where fairness is critical, yet often overlooked, including plan design, documentation, budgeting, target allocation, administration, and governance. From the novice to the expert, this book will become a quick favorite to ensuring all bases are covered in executing a fair, and equitable, sales compensation program.

— KATIE P.

Christopher Goff methodically and intentionally sets up a clear and concise path to help the reader understand the complexities of fairness and how it can be achieved in any organization. This book is a must read for any sales or team leader who is committed to the principles of fairness. The author provides guidance throughout the book with examples, checklists and stories on how to lay the groundwork of fairness... and how the internal culture of the organization can impact fairness at all levels.

— JAN H.

As a Sales Compensation professional, I agree with Chris's suggestions on using historical data to try and avoid bias around your sales compensation program. Chris's examples in the book show how easily this can happen without intention. This book is a great resource for Sales Managers/Ops teams to read so they can check *themselves when setting up quotas and taking the personal aspects out of quota setting.*

    — SALLY W.

I think it is a great high-level tool to start thinking philosophically about how to shape a sales compensation program or a tool that can be used in companies with existing programs to determine if their current plan is hitting the mark. While not an exact recipe that a company can follow, in my mind the book can be used to serve as the foundation to outline the major components of a sales comp program and to get companies thinking about the look and more importantly the feel of an ethical program that mirrors the overall company vision. I felt like the book put the big and important things first.

    — REBECCA P.

Sales Compensation

When you don't know where to begin or what you even need, Starting Simple is simply the best place to start. Chris brings his many years of experience, insights and proven strategies to start your sales compensation program. From identifying your needs to how to get there, this should be the only resource your need. This book is based on proven strategies rather than subjective theories. Simply start by Starting Simple. You will enjoy this straight to the point, easy read to get you on the road to success!

— LAUREN F.

Starting Simple is a quick read, offering practical and reliable insights. Author has a way of simplifying difficult subject matter and offers meaningful insights for nearly any organization either established or in the process of being a startup. The book excels at offering up solid points for consideration while making the content enjoyable and approachable for readers. I enjoyed the book and would recommend to anyone in the sales compensation process.

– RON S.

You can read all about creating a sales compensation plan, but having step-by-step exercises to help you gather everything you need to start creating your plan is invaluable. This workbook is an excellent, one-of-a-kind resource and action plan for getting your comp plan off the ground.

– ABBY L.

This is such a great book for those who are starting from scratch and launching their own business. I appreciate the value the author places on avoiding pitfalls when setting up an appropriate sales strategy and incentive structure for the small business owner. More importantly, I'm grateful for the "step-by-step" approach: do your homework first, in order to accomplish your objectives successfully. I highly recommend this book!

– KELLEY S.

I have had many sales roles in my career, and now- as a sales leader, I can appreciate the complex decisions that need to be made when you are creating a compensation plan. As the title suggests, Goff makes selecting measures and compensation simple for the leader and, more importantly, for the salesperson. I have personally seen Goff's process work extremely well.

    – DILLON D.

Written in clear, concise language. Great for anyone who wants a greater understanding of how compensation works.

    – JOHN H.

Pay Transparency: Readying Your Organization for Pay Equity Legislation

A well-thought out and well-written guide to understanding the potential impact of pay transparency on your organization. Whether you like it or not, pay transparency is here to stay and this book easily guides you through the steps you can start taking today to ensure you are properly prepared to report your Company pay statistics. This book is educational, yet entertaining - it's hard to put down once you pick it up! Would recommend this read to individuals at all career levels, from entry-level positions to 15+ years in professional compensation.

– Katherine B.

A great read for those that are not experienced compensation consultants but also a great read for us that are experienced consultants. He does an excellent job of outlining the new rules, in a meaningful and engaging way!! He shares employer insights as they relate to current and future state. I would not miss out on the opportunity to better understand pay transparency; Pick this book up today and you will not regret it!!!

— BRITTANY S.

As a business owner, this is valuable information presented in a very clear and pragmatic way. Thank you for the insights on what to pay attention to and how to handle it! Well done!

— QUINN T.

Christopher explains the implications of pay transparency laws that are popping up across several states. There is a focus on CA and NY, with clearly articulated advice for companies to be ready. His ability to tackle a seemingly complex topic in a simple, easy-to-understand language make this a very quick and informative read. Highly recommend.

— PRASAD V.

An excellent quick read that encourages the reader to embrace pay transparency. Further, offers clear, concise steps to consider while navigating potential issues. As the author reminds us – the time is now to get ahead of the wave.

— K.C.

Table of Contents

Table of Contents

Foreword

By Karen Heier
SVP, Global Sales

Finding top sales talent is what keeps sales leaders up at night. Great hires can boost your business and have a meaningful impact on your company's success, while mediocre or wrong hires can not only can have a neutral/ negative effect but can also impact the sales team's morale.

It has been my great pleasure as a forty-year sales professional with twenty years in sales leadership to work with Chris for the last five years as our sales compensation specialist. Chris brings unique and balanced ideas to our team to guide us in offers for hiring talent, rewarding performance, and retaining talent in our competitive sales environment. Chris' qualifications include multiple advanced degrees and certifications in the areas of compensation, as well as extensive experience in sales operations, incentive design, and running compensation programs globally for over 18 years.

Hiring for Sales is an easy read with practical recommendations for each step of the hiring process. It begins with thoughts on how to assess whether a new hire is needed and completes the journey with tips to effectively onboard the talent. It also includes tips on how to retain talent and great guidance on whether engaging an agency makes sense for your success.

Whether you seek great ideas on crafting your job description or interviewing questions (where he recommends using behavioral questions to predict future performance, which I have found most valuable in interviewing sales candidates), this book can be read to upskill on the entire hiring process or used at the chapter level for specific needs in your organization.

Thanks to Chris for providing this easily digestible guide based on proven experience for the most critical skill needed by sales leadership!

Introduction:
How to Use this Book

Every success story is a tale of constant adaption, revision and change. A company that stands still will soon be forgotten.

- Sir Richard Branson

To improve is to change; to be perfect is to change often.

- Winston Churchill

A colleague recently shared a story with me. Her organization sells enterprise-level software contracts to large hospitals and health systems, and they were considering getting into the post-acute care market.

She'd been toying with the idea of a shift in territory planning based not only on geography but on the market segment as well. However, it was just an idea that she hadn't put the research into. So, when Bill, an expert in sales in the post-acute market, showed up, she hesitated because she and her team were nowhere near ready to make such an investment or change to their territory plans. Still, it seemed too good an opportunity to pass up, so she decided to hire him and see what he could do.

As it turned out, Bill did know—or believed he knew—the post-acute health market very well. He knew it so well that whenever my colleague presented ideas to him or asked him to push the limits a bit, he refused on the basis that he knew what would and wouldn't sell. Unfortunately, she had no way of knowing whether his limitations were self-inflicted or were the result of superior knowledge because she hadn't done market research before executing pressure tests in the new market.

The situation didn't turn out well for anyone. Bill didn't perform well and parted ways with the organization, and my colleague's team lost months of time and resources on an experiment that hadn't been properly prepared for.

So, what's the point of this story? I suppose it's to set up the reason behind this book. Hiring for sales requires due diligence, and without it, you can end up facing some pretty dire consequences (just wait until you get to chapter 5).

Who is this book for, exactly? For anyone hiring a salesperson – as the title suggests! Whether you're leading the process, involved, or being hired, this book will be of value to you. This is also for every small or mid-sized sales organization that needs to be in tune with the roles that support and acquire revenue for the organization. It can be a rigorous, heavily involved process, or it can be simple and seamless. Your organization will differ from others.

Not many people leaders would call themselves "professional interviewers." However, it would be a mistake to go through the process of hiring without leaning on the proven learnings of experienced sales leaders.

You can find lots of books on hiring and interviewing, and while many of the skills in those books are transferable, there are some special considerations to make when hiring specifically for sales. One of those considerations is your sales compensation program, which is likely more complex than the compensation for other non-sales roles in your organization. If nothing more, it is important to define, document, and then communicate the coverage model, job responsibilities, quota assignment, and sales opportunity, amongst other aspects.

In my first book, *Starting Simple: Sales Compensation*, I go over the process of forming (or revamping) a sales compensation structure for any organization. I highly recommend including that in your reading—preferably before hiring for that sales role.

Additionally, be sure to have your financials in order before posting a role or building a job description. It's essential to the stability of the function.

You may be tempted to skip around in this book or to go straight to the interview chapter. If you're new to hiring or only do it occasionally, I strongly recommend you read in order and use the exercises and concepts to revisit sections in each chapter to set yourself up for long-term success. This is a case of small investments today, saving you frustration and clean-up time in the future. If you are a sales hiring pro, feel free to take the parts and pieces separately and as needed. Each chapter can be consumed separately and in its entirety.

If you are unfamiliar with sales functions but are responsible for bringing on or building a sales team, be sure to use the other resources I have available at www.salescompguy.com.

The first chapter is about whether or not to hire, and you may be thinking, "Well, of course, I'm ready to hire; otherwise, why did I pick up this book?" Read it anyway. This may not apply to you, but there are plenty of people who've been directed to hire by leadership or individually think they are ready to expand their sales team but haven't truly thought through all of the consequences and impact of the needed decisions for this kind of organization move. This may sound odd, but just because you have an open position doesn't mean it's the best time to hire.

The rest of the book takes you through the broader talent acquisition process, from defining your role to attracting candidates to hiring and retaining talent. Throughout the book, there are also reminders to align your strategy and cultural values with these many different points of consideration throughout that sales hiring process. But not every step is in what you might consider the traditional order. A lot of research has been done around interviewing and retention in particular, and many hiring managers have discovered better ways of asking questions and attracting the right candidates.

Lastly, I want to say that if you're new to hiring, and even if you've done it many times before, the process is not easy and very often uncomfortable. From experience, I know the grueling amount of work and detail that goes into it, and my aim is to help simplify the experience for you while also making sure you don't miss any of the more vital steps in the process.

As always, I'm happy to answer any questions or help in any way I can. If you read this book and would like to talk more about hiring for sales, don't hesitate to reach out to me at <u>christopher@salescompguy.com</u>.

Chapter 1:
To Hire or Not To Hire

*Change the way you look at things and
the things you look at change.*

- WAYNE DYER

An objective without a plan is a dream.

- DOUGLAS MCGREGOR

Have you ever had a product or service that just sold itself? Not many of us have experienced that, but one organization did. They came out with the right product at the right time, and orders flowed in with zero need for sales and a robust customer service team running the show.

But then, out of nowhere, the orders stopped. Maybe the market shifted, or maybe the demand changed. The reasons are less important than the lesson. At this point, the organization was in danger of folding unless they could put together a successful sales team quickly.

It's worth speculating whether the organization did anything wrong. Should they have invested in a sales team when it didn't appear to be needed? Or did they actually do the right thing at the moment before being forced to adapt? Could market research have helped them to predict and prepare for the future? Did they have other options besides hiring for sales?

Your organization has its own unique quirks and needs, but since this is a book on hiring a salesperson, the question everyone should have to answer is: Are you sure you need to hire a salesperson?

This is a question you should be asking yourself regardless of whether you're hiring your first salesperson, your seventeenth, or filling a newly vacated position. And the answer is more complex than you might think.

Is now the right time to hire for sales?

1. Determine whether your organization is experiencing or on the verge of

experiencing growth. The importance comes in the "how" or the "what way" that it is expected to occur.

2. Investigate other options besides hiring a salesperson. What are the alternatives? For example, could you adjust the responsibilities of your current roles? Or perhaps allocate expected growth opportunities differently?

3. Get clear on your organization's financials and if adding headcount will help or hinder the financial position.

The Growth Potential

Two words that are sometimes mistakenly used interchangeably are growth and scale. It's important to differentiate between the two because it can affect when and how you hire.

An easy way to differentiate between the two is this:

- If we start with a financial point of view, growth is the expansion at the same rate. As an example, think of expanded revenue at the same margin. Scaling is about improving the margins (generally through cost reduction or through price increases). Scaling adds value to the organization at each incremental dollar (or product sold).

- Growth is the starting point after which you may begin to scale. At the point of experiencing positive growth, it's time to begin strategically supporting that growth through activities that can allow the organization to scale.

- Scaling is what you eventually want to do in response to growth, not what you do to try and prompt growth.

- Scaling can be done in other ways beyond the financial purview, such as adding value to the organization. Areas like internal processes, licensing restructure, and intellectual property investments can all add value incrementally to the organization.

For example, back in 2006, a little company called Wise Acre Treats that produced organic popsicles was making a big splash in the industry.

The product had won awards and was being received positively. As a result of what the owner perceived to be momentum, he hired 13 more employees and moved production into a massive factory. The owner anticipated that the awards would naturally encourage consumers to accept higher prices.

Unfortunately, because his attempt to scale was done to spur growth, he didn't have the financial requisites to successfully carry this off, and the company went bankrupt. Sadly, these actions were taken prior to stable and consistent cash-flow and revenue levels. While we will never know, there likely would have been an opportunity to scale had the owner waited for growth in demand before scaling, but he jumped the gun to the detriment of his business.

Expansion occurs when your company's revenue increases at the same or similar rate as the cost of resources it takes to acquire that revenue. The result is growth in size but not in marginal value. You've basically just become a bigger version of what you already are. Scaling occurs when you grow in revenue and improve margins (or reduce costs), thereby expanding the marginal and overall value of your organization. It is important to note that improvement in the financials is not the same as growth.

What does this have to do with hiring a salesperson? Why do I need to know this when bringing on an additional employee? It's because an incremental employee, especially in sales, is a costly endeavor. You have to make sure your growth in revenue can at least compensate for the expense of hiring, onboarding, and retaining a new salesperson. Will that be accomplished in your proposed headcount expansion? If so, for how long with limited or no attributable performance by the salesperson?

Ideally, the organization will want to scale after the initial levels of growth. Will you be able to do that? Maybe your growth potential is such that you can scale even while hiring a salesperson, but we won't really know that until we get into some math. So, let's look at other factors that play into growth. From here on out, we're going to use a fictional company to help illustrate the ideas in this book. That company is called Greenville Gadgets, and they manufacture—you guessed it--gadgets. We are also going to utilize USD, represented by '$' in most of the examples. The mathematical concepts should translate across currencies, but it is easier to stay in one form throughout.

Capacity: This is how much business you're delivering right now—it's everything from the number of gadgets you're producing, how fast you're able to produce them, and the labor time costs, raw materials, and marketing and sales budget it takes to get them to market, and ultimately revenue. To determine your potential for either expansion or scale, you need to take a look at your operations and compare your current capacity to your potential capacity.

There's a clever claymation cartoon called Shaun the Sheep that illustrates this idea perfectly. In the first episode, Shaun appropriates the farmer's kiln to start making pizzas. At first, he's just feeding himself and the other farm animals, but pretty soon, customers begin lining up and holding out their cash. Shaun makes the decision to go into business. He brings on some employees (other sheep), creates some automation like a conveyor belt for moving the pizza crust along a pizza assembly line, and uses old boxes for packaging.

Pretty soon, Shaun had a thriving business, but demand quickly increased. This situation is the opposite of the Wise Acre Frozen Treats scenario, in which they scaled too soon. In Shaun's case, the growth potential was there, but the capacity wasn't. His equipment began failing because it couldn't keep up with the increased speed. His employees began performing poorly. At one point, the sheep in charge of keeping the fire in the oven ran out of wood and began burning the barrel full of cash they no longer had any use for.

That image of an organization literally burning its cash to keep production going is the perfect example of a capacity problem.

And this is sometimes what trips people up. You don't want to invest in more capacity if you haven't established the potential for growth; however, if growth occurs, you want to be prepared, in terms of capacity, to take on more work. It's a tricky thing to navigate and requires some important considerations, such as:

- Increased load (orders, sales, inputs) doesn't inherently mean increased profit. There are scenarios where the cost of increasing the load dramatically narrows the profit margin—in some cases, eliminating it altogether. So you have to ask yourself, how can your organization increase the load in a cost-effective way that doesn't narrow your profit margin?

- Salespeople sell. So, if you're looking to grow your consumer base, hiring a salesperson can be a great investment. However, make sure your organization has the capacity to meet the new levels of demand so that you can continue to deliver at the same quality as expected. There's no sense in simply trading the lose of existing customers for new customers because of internal limitations.

- Things can get frantic during times of growth and scaling. But don't give into the pace. It's far more valuable to approach business evolutions, including any hiring you do at this time, from a calm, process-and-plan-driven approach. Make sure quality changes are proactive for shaping your future, not reactive in response to the feeling of urgency in a hectic moment.

💡 Take a break to really look at your capacity. How much more could you do with the same resources, time & labor, and budget? What would it look like to increase one or all of those factors? Assuming you were able to sell at your maximum capacity, would your organization be in a state of loss, growth, or scaling?

Demand: Customer demand is one of those factors you don't always have a clear picture of. But look at your existing process. If those gadgets are selling out as soon as they hit the market, you definitely have an unmet customer demand, which is a good problem to have. However, if the gadgets are sitting on the shelves, you likely have one of two problems: either consumers don't want it, or consumers don't know about it – or even worse, both. You should be able to access customer feedback from reviews or customer support tickets to help you know if it's the former. If it's the latter, you have a marketing and sales problem—which may (or may not) be an indicator that it's time to hire a salesperson. The best product in the world is useless if the world doesn't know about it.

*Note: This is a far more complicated topic to address related to the manufacturing, logistics, distribution, and procurement to get an object to market. When we take a look at capacity, we don't want to forget to assess the capacity of the existing sales functions (and other roles) from the standpoint of clarity of the job, productivity, and evolution of the job responsibilities. Have you taken the time to assess sales capacity to expand or scale to supply and respond to follow through on the demand in the market? Without this opportunity, sales and expansion of the salesforce have little to no capability to be successful.

Expectations: These are your financial obligations. How will the fixed and variable costs be impacted by expanding with a new sales employee? Do you have investors to answer to? Loans to pay off? If so, that raises the stakes on how you manage your growth. In order to not be redundant, the reason expectations are called out is simply to add the financial obligations to the points already made related to internal and external environments for a holistic picture of the current state of the organization for decision-making purposes.

Given these factors, determine what your growth or scaling potential financial moves are as an organization. Next, we'll talk about determining whether hiring a salesperson is the right next step in reaching organizational goals.

💡 Set your organizational goal based on the realities of the present moment and the evidence-based possibility of the future. Do you have the capacity and demand to grow within your existing framework? Do you want to set yourself up merely for growth, or are you looking to scale? Is your existing sales process working, sustainable, and repeatable? Ask yourself, is this a growth scenario (expansion at similar levels) or a scalability scenario (productivity gains)?

Don't Hire Unless You Have To

According to SHRM's new benchmarking data, hiring a new employee can cost you up to 40% of their annual base pay plus benefits.[1] For organizations of any size, it can be assumed that this isn't a negligible expense. If you pay $60,000 per year in base pay and have benefit costs of 22%, that translates into costs of at least $29,280. And that doesn't take into account any contributions (or failings) of the individual being hired into that job. The stakes are high for this decision.

To further complicate matters, studies show that the turnover rate for sales employees is 27%, more than double the turnover rate in other employee roles.[2] Additionally, according to the Bureau of Labor Statistics, the average total actual compensation of a field-based sales resource selling technical or scientific products in the US is around $113K.[3] If we add in at least 20% for fringe, you can easily see that the high level of turnover and recruitment costs add up. The pressure is on to get it right. So, let's be sure we set up the salesperson for success.

You're taking on a lot of risk when hiring, and though we'll talk about mitigating that risk through preparation, it's also important to explore your options. One of those options is not to hire anyone right now. Can you achieve your next organizational goals without hiring a sales-person? If current demand outweighs existing operational output, the answer is easy. Yes. You can. To oversimplify, you just need to figure out how to increase capacity levels to meet the known demand levels – and help connect the consumer wants with your excess capacity.

On the other hand, if the current demand isn't there, you may still be able to meet the next organizational objective with your existing resources. This usually comes in one of two forms: shifting existing employee time and focus or trimming back operational areas that are expendable.[4] Ultimately, this is just a signal of caution given the magnitude of effort and expense wrapped up and associated with ill-timed decisions.

💡 Your objectives should include existing and projected market penetration. Run an analysis on business expansion using your existing resources versus using the addition of a new salesperson. Don't forget to account for the cost of hiring, ramp-up, and on-going costs of employment.

Of course, you have another alternative to hiring externally, and that is to promote from within. Statistics show that hiring managers are biased towards external hires in spite of the cost and retention problems associated with them. However, job progression, promotion, or role expansion are all possibilities to consider for meeting demand without expanding your headcount.

Ranking of Talent Sourcing by Corporate TA

Source	Percentage
Internal Candidate	28%
3rd Party Recruiters/Staffing Firm	34%
Social or Professional Networks	40%
3rd Party Websites/Job Boards	46%
Employee Referrals	48%

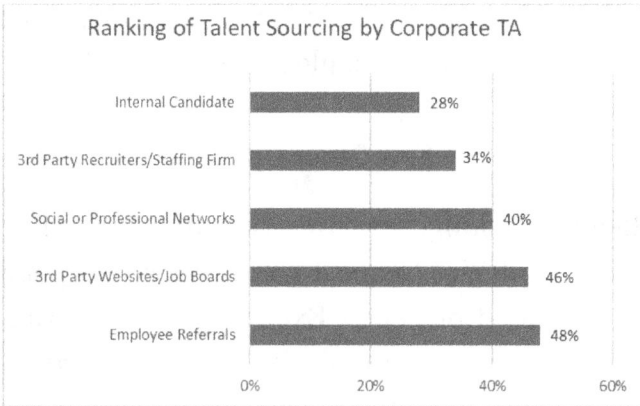

A recent survey from LinkedIn illustrated the bias towards looking externally to source talent. Is your future salesperson already sitting in your organization? [5]

Matthew Bidwell, Professor of Management at Wharton University of Pennsylvania, says that workers promoted into jobs generally perform better in the long term, are better culturally aligned, and are less expensive. [6]

Look to your existing talent, see if there's any interest, and consider training a salesperson within. While this isn't a free option, it's considerably less expensive and more reliable than hiring from the outside. If they are currently successful in their present role, then they already understand the cultural dynamics and strategy of the organization. And that alignment should not be undervalued.

A Few Other Options

Before deciding to hire, consider leveraging other strategies to boost your sales and expand your market presence. Exploring these alternatives can help you optimize resources, reduce costs, and potentially achieve better results without immediately increasing headcount.

Marketing Opportunities

One of the most effective ways to drive sales without hiring additional personnel is to enhance your marketing efforts. Investing in targeted marketing campaigns can attract potential customers and generate leads. Utilize digital marketing techniques such as search engine optimization (SEO), pay-per-click (PPC) advertising, content marketing, and social media engagement to reach a wider audience. By increasing brand awareness and creating compelling value propositions, you can stimulate interest and demand for your products or services. If you are currently investing in these areas, consider an optimization exercise for improved returns.

Automation

Automation tools can significantly streamline your sales processes and reduce the need for a large sales team. Customer Relationship Management (CRM) systems, email marketing automation, and chatbots can handle repetitive tasks, manage customer interactions, and nurture leads through the sales funnel. By automating routine activities, your existing team can focus on high-value tasks such as closing deals and building relationships, thereby increasing overall efficiency and productivity. This, of course, starts with existing processes. Note: If the current sales process is weak, no amount of technology will deliver better results.

Partnerships and Business Development

Forming strategic partnerships and exploring business development opportunities can also serve as an alternative to hiring a salesperson. Collaborate with complementary businesses to cross-promote products and services or establish reseller agreements. Third-party sales channels, such as distributors or affiliates, can expand your reach without the need to hire and manage additional staff. Additionally, partnering with brand ambassadors or industry experts can enhance your credibility and visibility in the market.

All of these options are intended to bring about consumer awareness and greater omnichannel exposure in the marketplace. They certainly can be done with a salesperson as well, but it may be more cost-effective to start here before hiring.

What Can You Afford?

I give a detailed walkthrough on how to determine what your organization can afford to pay a new salesperson in chapter two of my book _Starting Simple: Sales Compensation_. But here are a few of the highlights.

You need to do the math to determine whether you're able to pay a salesperson now or whether you're betting on your salesperson to cover their costs while increasing your revenue. If your organization is currently profitable to the tune of more than it will cost you to hire and retain a salesperson, then you're all set.

However, if you're hovering at break-even and you're hiring a salesperson to help you grow, you need to look at the gap between your targeted revenue and your current revenue levels. Obviously, you won't have that amount of money as soon as your salesperson starts selling. It will take time. But you can use that number to determine what you can afford in terms of guaranteed compensation.

Consider this: according to The Bridge Group's SDR Metrics and Comp Report of 2020, the average tenure of SDRs is 1.8 years, and the average ramp-up time is 3.1 months.[7] That nets to around 18 months of productivity at most. More senior sales roles may carry longer tenures but still have very high attrition rates. With this knowledge, how will the sales contribution play out in your organization?

Once you've determined base pay (guaranteed compensate), it's time to look at variable pay. Variable pay or pay-at-risk needs to be thought through both in terms of the organization's objective and the value of each transaction:

- Are some transactions being sold by the salesperson less valuable than others (whether in size, scope, profitability, etc.)?

- What is each marginal sale worth to the organization?

- What is the salesperson's role in procuring it?

- What can you afford to pay the salesperson at varying levels of performance?

These questions may seem overwhelming but taking the time to address them one by one can help determine the breadth and depth of the variable pay levels for a sustainable compensation plan that can evolve as your company grows.

A note on market research--I recommend it. But I recommend **starting with what you can afford** because market value is a moot point if your organization simply doesn't have the funds to pay.

More on market competitiveness in chapter three.

One More Thing

Thus far we've focused on whether you *can* hire a salesperson and whether you *should* hire a salesperson. However, there is one less data-driven factor that also comes into play.

As an employer in a small business, non-profit, or even as a solo entrepreneur, you've likely spent a lot of time being your own salesperson. Are you successful and consistent in business development? Do you enjoy that aspect of the business? If the answer to either of those questions is a "no," then factor that into your decision because it matters if you are building or expanding the sales team.

Don't be a martyr. If you can take off one of the many hats you wear and pass it to someone who is more qualified and who has the time and energy, do it. It's all part of growing a business. Gallup studies regularly show that teams that operate to their strengths have better productivity than those that don't.[8]

In the next chapter, we'll talk about defining the role of your future salesperson.

Concepts to Revisit

- Think about your next organizational target. Are you looking to scale? Or will you be satisfied with growth at the same rate?

- What is your capacity? Are you optimally structured with all the resources you have? Could you do more?

- Compare a projection of your capabilities for penetrating the market as you are against your capabilities with a new sales hire.

💡 Keep in mind that sales rep turnover is more than double the average turnover rate of other roles, and the average tenure is 18 months—are you prepared to experience that?

Chapter 2:
Defining the Role

To succeed in sales, simply talk to lots of people every day. And here's what's exciting – there are lots of people!

- JIM ROHN

Clarity precedes success.

- ROBIN SHARMA

In 2013, rumors began circulating that Wells Fargo employees in California were using potentially unethical sales tactics to meet their quotas for cross-selling.[9] Cross-selling is an important sales focus, especially in the financial sector, that involves selling additional products and services to existing customers.

Investigations found that in order to meet the aggressive cross-selling quotas, employees were opening up debit card accounts, credit cards, and lines of credit in customers' names without their knowledge. After numerous layoffs and a full investigation into the affected accounts, the company found that the economic and financial impact was small for both Wells Fargo and its customers, but the damage to its reputation was significant. And the courts would follow-through with penalties of around $3.7 billion for all of these fraudulent actions.

Apparently, the company had published performance scorecards that included cross-selling as a metric, placing undue pressure on employees to perform. Additionally, they openly admitted that their incentive plans were unattainable in nearly every region.

So, what does all of this have to do with a book chapter on defining a sales role? Everything.

In his book *Compensating the Sales Force*, David Cichelli defines an effective sales job as having "focus, clarity of purpose, and a clearly identified point of persuasion responsibility."[10] While the statement may sound simple enough, upon closer inspection, you can find plenty of points for potential failure. As the Wells Fargo example shows, any misalignment between job content and incentive design can result in disaster. The Wells Fargo example illustrated the behavioral side effects of heightened focus on intentionally unachievable performance expectations.

Job content is how we define a sales role. It isn't to be mistaken for the job description, which contains job content. The job content covers much of the basic commercial needs within your organization and is organized by defining the skills, knowledge, and abilities necessary for a salesperson to meet and exceed those needs.

Job content is the outline of the role and responsibilities of the position. It can be simple or complex based on the job functions. The content of the job describes what, how, where, and when. It may even describe the who and the why. A good job description provides clarity for the applicant and your future growth.

Examples of Job Descriptions

At this point, you've determined you need to hire a salesperson. You've done the work and found that a salesperson in the right role with the right incentives can not only pay for their existence in the organization but also lead to incremental profitable outcomes. Remember, you're not just hiring to fill a vacancy. Each salesperson (as well as non-sales role) that is being hired into the organization is intended to fill a very real need at this specific point in time. That has real risk and real reward attached to it.

In my first book, _Starting Simple: Sales Compensation_, I warn against taking shortcuts by leaning on sites like Monster or Indeed to build your job descriptions. Because you are hiring for a very specific need, it's going to pay off to put the effort into defining this role from scratch – specific to your organization's unique culture and strategy at this moment in time. You'll want to have answers to questions like:

- What does the person need to do on a daily basis?

- How does this individual pursue sales, and in what segment or with what type of customer?

- Where should they focus their time and attention on building a pipeline of deals?

- Who should they be interfacing with, both internally and externally?

- When do they engage with customers and/or prospects?

This is where you want to start documenting your job.

Your salesperson's day-to-day

When thinking about the new salesperson, imagine what a day in their life is going to look like. Will they be making phone calls? If so, are they responsible for gathering leads? Are they responsible for closing sales on the phone, or is that just part of a longer sales process? Maybe your salesperson will be doing more in-person selling. Will they be responsible for scheduling these meetings? If the sale is a long-term process, how much of it will your salesperson be involved in?

Chances are your salesperson won't be externally customer-facing for the entire eight-hour workday, so what else will they be doing? If your organization is on the smaller side, you might need them to wear a few hats, with sales being their main role. However, aspects of the job will likely include compliance, administration, and support requirements, such as time-tracking, populating trip documentation, populating expense reports, CRM management, and helping clients reconcile invoices, support tickets, or billing concerns.

Picturing a day in the life of your salesperson will help you frame reasonable expectations. It will also help you picture the behaviors and traits you want in your new hire.

In his book, *The Effective Hiring Manager*, Mark Horstman encourages hiring managers to shift their mindset from thinking about traits to thinking about behaviors. So, instead of looking for someone who is creative, look for someone who behaves creatively. He says, "The best way to interview someone, then, is to look for behaviors that are necessary and sufficient for success in our role, and which the person has engaged in previously."[11]

As you imagine your salesperson interacting with their client, think about the words they use, their facial expressions and body language, the quality of their work, and other words that demonstrate competence and success in your eyes.

🔆 Write down the behaviors that you want to see in your salesperson's interactions with coworkers and customers. Then, write down the behaviors you don't want to see. This will help you interview with clarity later on and not compromise with any "gut" feelings you might have about subtle behavioral cues.

Sales, Segments, and Customers

How will your salesperson pursue sales? The answer to this question depends on the type of sales they will be engaged in. There are potentially hundreds of different sales jobs, and not all of them have to do with carrying a briefcase and meeting with clients on the road, in-person, or face-to-face.

According to Cichelli, there are six sales job segments, including income producers, direct sales jobs, indirect sales jobs, overlay sales jobs, business development, and pre- and post-sales support.[12] Each of these segments is about the customer's position and how the seller will interact to support the buying process. Is your new salesperson going to work with new prospective accounts or existing customers?

Clearly identifying the sales segment your new hire will work in is essential to drafting the content of the role. If you don't take the time to do this, you run the risk of weakening your job design in a way that could result in overloading your salesperson with too many responsibilities or failing to give them clear direction. Attempting to do everything often leads very quickly to doing nothing at all.

What to Focus On

Similar to identifying the customer type or sale job segment, you also need to identify where your salesperson is going to focus their attention in order to best benefit the company.

You may have a product with a short sales process that can be managed from start to finish by a single salesperson. They contact the lead, negotiate with the lead, and contract with the lead.

But if your sales process is longer, it's likely necessary to position your salesperson with ownership of a portion of the sales process where they have a simple, clear, and impactful job to do. Maybe this is working in the later stages of the sales process, including closing transactions.

Maybe it's nurturing a lead to the point of final commitment and then handing them off internally for final negotiation and contracting.

💡 In startups and smaller organizations, salespeople often have to fulfill multiple roles. Even if this is the case, map out your sales plan and market opportunity. Look at where the burden of the sales process falls now. Rather than trying to hire for the entire sales process, pick the points on the map where a sales representative can create the greatest impact, recognizing that this may evolve over time – especially if the salesperson is quickly successful in that function.

Who To Talk To?

Who your salesperson interacts with, both internally and externally, factors into what the "size" or "level" of the role will be. Who will their direct supervisor be? Who will they work with on the team? Are they reporting to a mid-level sales manager or as high up as the CEO?

What about customers? When they go to pitch your product or service, who are they talking to? Is it the executive staff or the procurement manager, or are buying decisions made directly by business management or consumers?

As a rule, it's a good idea to define the job role with a level of seniority commensurate with the level of the job they are expected to persuade and influence. Examples of job levels in sales ranked from lowest to highest are usually associate, representative, senior representative, and account executive. An account executive is going to communicate with high-level decision-makers. A sales associate will probably be reporting to more senior sales staff. In other organizations, those levels may look more like Associate Manager, Manager, Sr Manager, Director, Sr Director, Vice President, Sr. Vice President, and Executive Vice President, etc.

Keep in mind that the level of the role affects the market value. If your budget is along the lines of being able to hire an associate-level sales representative, but you need someone who can sit across the table from senior executives, you will need to get creative with your compensation plan and total rewards program. More on that later.

Right now, let's focus on what you need. Think about who your salesperson is going to be communicating with and use that as a guide to deciding the level of the position.

Engaging with Customers

At what point does your salesperson engage with customers or prospects? Generally, the customer journey may go something like this:

Awareness
Consideration
Purchase
Service/Support
Advocacy

Of course, yours will vary from this, but it is important to recognize what client experience you are hoping to achieve and how you want the salesperson to guide the prospective or existing client through. Where on that map do you want your salesperson to engage with the customer? The answer to this question is going to decide how your salesperson engages (emails, cold calls, virtual conference calls, webinars, conference booths, face-to-face meetings, etc.) and also what level or levels of customers they intend to interact with.

While there may be times that you have a salesperson managing the entire customer journey, you want to try to keep their focus as simple and clean as possible. An inside salesperson generating warm leads partnered with a field-based representative who focuses on converting those leads and a client success manager who keeps up with service and support needs all collaboratively working together is likely better than a single salesperson running themselves into the ground trying to manage it all. Defined hand-off and internal collaboration processes, role accountability, and clarity of work responsibilities are keys to success.

Time for Market Research

Let's say you've designed your job content, and you've already written a job description. You're looking for a mid-level sales representative because the people who make the decisions about whether to buy your gadget are product managers and directors for mid-sized businesses. You want your salesperson to develop relationships with already established leads and walk them up to the point of decision.

Now, it's time to do some market research. Look for comparable roles using the following free resources to see what the going market pay is for your new role:

- <u>www.bls.gov</u> Under the Occupational Employment and Wage Statistics section, you can see the actual pay details for various occupations. It is a good starting point.

- <u>https://www.onetonline.org/</u> is a good resource for developing job content and seeing how that job content is aligned with a particular job title. The great thing about this database is that you can get started with a simple search on "sales" to view all of the different occupations that align with that keyword.

- <u>www.repvue.com</u> is a repository for SaaS sales jobs. They collect their data in partnership with companies to manage recruitment and collect data from individuals to supplement the ranking of organizations in that sector. If you are sourcing talent from the software/technology sector, these are the pay levels that you will need to be aware of. This will aid in both the pay amounts and the job description elements.

- <u>https://www.payscale.com/products/</u>
  <u>payfactors-free/</u> is a 100% HR-sourced,
  employer-validated compensation database. You can get started by market pricing a couple of jobs for free and can use
  your specific industry or location.

There are plenty of surveys and resources that
include posting sites themselves. Leverage
everything you can because that's where your
talent will be looking as well.

A Note on Internal Equity and Pay Transparency

Market value and your budget aren't the only
factors in decisions about how to pay your new
salesperson. You also have to take into account
what you're already paying your existing team
members. The new hire's pay levels need to fit
reasonably within your already existing pay
scales or within some predefined range — this
consideration for consistency of pay is called
internal equity.

Depending on where you live, you may already
have put in the time to build out your standard-
ized pay bands and provide transparent ranges.
However, as of the writing of this book, there

are still a lot of states that don't have pay transparency laws. The reality is that those laws are coming, and you'll be in better shape when they do if you work on standardizing your compensation programs.

Now, back to internal equity. You want to make sure that the pay offered to your new salesperson is commensurate with the job level, years of experience, education, and type of work they're going to be doing. And, in making that decision of the pay to offer, that the pay level is commensurate with other existing employees' pay levels for similar work being done, years of experience, and education, amongst other aspects. The goal is to remove potential inequities intentionally – with some method for determining the amount of pay offered consistently.

💡 Once you've gathered market data and analyzed the pay ranges in your own company, go ahead and try your hand at updating your job description. You may have learned that you need to upgrade or downgrade the language to align with your needs and budget.

Pitching to the Higher-Ups

Another advantage to doing all this pre-work is that you'll be ready to support your request if you need to get approval for hiring.

In one case, a hiring manager needed to bring on six new field salespeople, an expensive incremental request for the business to absorb. Knowing the cost of hiring these six people, she knew she had to present a strong argument for the value they would bring.

This meant preparing the financial expectations and making a clear commitment to the organization to deliver results. That also meant she spent extra time doing some research into what the leadership wanted to hear and prepared to commit to taking responsibility for the outcomes and/or consequences should the decision be accepted.

The bolder the request, the higher the risk. That means it's especially important to do your due diligence, putting in the time to research the cost/value of a new hire and developing a hiring process that can protect you and your organization in the future. More on that in chapter five.

Concepts to Revisit

💡 Write down the behaviors that you want to see in your salesperson's interactions with coworkers and customers. Then, write down the behaviors you don't want to see. This will help you interview with clarity later on and not compromise with any "gut" feelings you might have about subtle behavioral cues.

💡 Salespeople often have to fulfill multiple roles. Even if this is the case, map out your sales process. Look at where the burden of sales ownership falls. Rather than trying to hire for the entire sales process, pick the point on the map where a new sales representative can create the greatest impact the fastest.

💡 Take the time to document the role responsibilities and expectations of the job. Be sure to make it unique to your organization. Resist the urge to copy from Indeed or LinkedIn and write your description from scratch. Don't be afraid to infuse some personality into it—this will give your prospective hire a feel for the tone and culture of your workplace.

💡 Once you've gathered market data and reviewed the internal pay ranges in your own company, go ahead back to your job description and see if you need to modify it based on what you can afford.

Chapter 3:
Competitive Assessment

*The most expensive thing you can do in sales
is to spend your time with the wrong prospect.*

- JOB BLOUNT

*Start with good people, lay out the rules,
communicate with your employees,
motivate them and reward them. If you do
all those things effectively, you can't miss.*

- LEE IACOCCA

As of the writing of this book, there are 11 states with pay transparency laws and another ten states proposing legislation. That means that data is coming into the public eye, and you are required to provide the pay expectations of the role you're hiring for. That means posting pay levels for new hires and providing pay data, upon request, for existing employees.

Pay transparency laws have a lot of implications for organizations, but for the purposes of this chapter, we're going to focus on how to use that growing cultural expectation in conjunction with other resources to assess the market competitiveness of the job you defined in the last chapter. Before we get started, let's talk about compensable factors.

Compensable Factors

Compensable factors are distinct characteristics of the job that elevate or reduce the value of the job in the labor market. These same factors are what will differentiate the level of the job. Compensable factors include items like industry experience, communication and presentation skills, level of autonomy and responsibility exercised, the complexity of duties, education and training, working conditions, supervision, or direction required.

Each of these helps you determine the level of the job to compare to in the marketplace. For example, if you're looking for someone with 5-10 years of experience and a master's degree, you're not going to be comparing your job description to entry-level positions.

The process of stacking up the compensable factors to evaluate a compensation amount is usually called job matching or market pricing. A similar process focused on internal levels and equity is called job evaluation.

💡 Make a list of compensable factors in your job description. What education and experience levels are you looking for? What are the working conditions your new hire will be expected to perform in? How much or how little supervision do you intend to give them?

Also, take note that analyzing your compensable factors also shows you where you can make adjustments if it turns out your role is a little out of your budget. If you have to make some concessions, where will you make them? Maybe you'll be willing to offer a little more internal training so that you can lower the education or experience requirements. Maybe you'd prefer to adjust the complexity of duties or the level of autonomy you originally expected.

You want the best person for the job, but sometimes you have to make some adjustments to your appetite, whether based on budget or the ability to provide appropriate levels of support and success.

Once you've got your compensable factors listed out, look through job listings that are similar to your role.

Types of Pay

In my first book, _Starting Simple: Sales Compensation_, I describe the components of a compensation plan, including total compensation and pay mix. You can read about them in more detail there. But for our purposes, here's an overview.

Components of a pay plan generally include base pay and variable pay. Variable pay generally comes in the form of a commission rate, bonus as a percentage of base pay, or a target sales incentive amount.

Pay mix refers to the amount of base pay relative to the total target cash compensation. For example, if a sales job has a salary of $40,000 and a variable pay target of $10,000, the job has an 80/20 mix - 80% base pay and 20% variable pay.

It's important to note that variable pay is also known as pay at risk, and that term comes into play when considering the offer you're going to make. A principle you'll want to follow is the idea that the higher the risk, the higher the potential for reward should be considered. For instance, if your sales position is 100% commission, you should make sure that the commission rate is a big enough payoff for the salesperson to put all their eggs in one basket. Meaning the expected level of performance is sizeable enough to deliver an appropriate level of total pay for the position.

💡 Pick five job descriptions that are similar to what you're looking for, ranging from the low end to the high end of the market pay spectrum. List out each of the following: base salary, variable pay, total target cash, and the core compensable factors provided in the data collected.

	High	Low	Targeted
Base Salary			
Variable Pay			
Total Target Cash Compensation			
Years of Sales Experience			
Total Years of Experience			
Education Level			
Other Compensable Factors Mentioned			

Sales Compensation Structure

Your sales compensation structure encompasses not just your total target cash compensation and pay mix but also how the variable pay is distributed. This includes determining the incentive total, what happens when the salesperson reaches 100% of the objective, when pay is disbursed, what the performance measurement period is, and other factors like pay under and over that targeted performance level.

All of these can change depending on the sales role you're hiring for. Here are a few categories to consider and how to compensate beyond the Department of Labor (DOL) requirements that differentiate the way field sales and inside sales are paid:

Field Sales vs. Inside Sales: In a field sales role, your salesperson is, by definition, expected to travel to meet the client face to face, although more recently, many more meetings can now be done virtually. An inside sales role doesn't travel (business travel is expected to be very limited).

New Client, Existing Client, Hybrid: Do you want your new sales hire to generate their own leads and establish prospect relationships, or do you want them to work toward closing deals with existing leads? Maybe you want them to do a little of both. These differences impact the total pay and pay mix because of the magnitude of risk.

Transactional vs. Complex: Is your sales rep selling a small-dollar product or supports a transactional sale? Or are they selling intricate services that require custom configuration and have long sales cycles? Generally, remuneration is related to the complexity of the product offering, speed of closure, or type of service being sold.

Small, Mid, or Enterprise Level Market: Who is your salesperson pursuing an audience with? Are you a direct-to-consumer organization or a business-to-business service provider? And if you're B2B or a non-profit securing funding, how big are the organizations you're trying to secure relationships from? What is the role's responsibility, the complexity of the sales process, market segment or size, length of sales cycle, coverage model, and level of decision-maker?

Generalist vs. Specialist: How complex is the product or service knowledge you offer? How technical is the messaging or configuration that is intended to be disseminated to the customer or prospect? I tend to ask whether a subject matter expert is needed before a sales function is required. We are talking about the percentage of the job that is a catalyst, informant, challenger, guide, etc., rather than a sales function. Does the sales process require multiple functions with varying points of technical expertise to ensure a successful outcome? They may not all be sales roles.

In each of these comparatives, take into consideration the level of knowledge and experience required, the amount of risk, and the final value contributed by the salesperson in the acquisition of business opportunities. These things will help inform how you structure your compensation.

For example, an inside salesperson who manages inbound lead qualification is an ideal candidate for a pay mix that would be 80% base pay with a 20% quota-based bonus. On the other hand, \field-based sales executives traveling to prospect sites and closing deals might prefer the opportunity for higher pay at risk and the potential for a large commission based on the size or complexity of the transactions. I'd expect the pay mix for the field-based role to be closer to 60% base and 40% variable.

Your Compensation Philosophy

This section arguably should come first, and it's especially important when we get into attracting a candidate. It is hard to know if you go down the right path on pay if you don't have a guiding principle of what or how you want to remunerate your employees. If there is no "true north," how do you know you are headed in the right direction?

It can be difficult when browsing all the resumés to get caught up in the justification of considering someone who might throw up red flags but has really amazing industry experience or an impressive Rolodex.

So, having a codified compensation philosophy helps you check your decisions against a firm foundation of who you want to be as an organization.

Compensation philosophy, according to Payscale, a compensation trends company, should consist of three things:

1. A plan for rewarding growth and success.

2. Determinants of pay, promotion, and equity distribution.

3. Breakdown of compensation.[13]

Every organization's compensation philosophy is going to depend on a variety of factors, including its culture, values, mission, and product or service. The important thing is to make sure that your philosophy is true and that you can hold true to it.

Here's an example:

As a young, scrappy organization, we value and reward creativity and problem-solving skills. While we offer less aggressive base pay, our variable pay program rewards those who put in the time, effort, and business contributions. In addition to base pay, our total compensation package includes employee-contributed healthcare, dental, vision, a 401k, a wellness program, and participation in ownership.

Additionally, if you believe it is necessary, you can also define your sales compensation philosophy statement. An example below:

As a professional services provider, we have to compete for and regularly win over different decision-makers at our existing clients daily. Our values, mission, and purpose must shine through in the relationships we maintain and in the support we provide to our customers daily. The organization puts emphasis on the acquisition of incremental revenue and generously rewards activities that align with that pursuit.

💡 *Write your compensation philosophy.*

Justin Hampton of CompTool aggregated an A-to-Z collection of compensation philosophies. His blog post titled "A Guide to Designing a Compensation Philosophy" is a great resource to utilize in your development of a philosophy statement. Not only does he provide examples, but he also outlines many of the aspects that should be addressed in that statement.[14]

With the compensation philosophy complete, let's go back to the job to see if our original intentions match up with our evolution of thought and philosophy and the market data we have collected.

How does your job stack up to the market?

💡 Does anything need to change about the job you previously defined? If so, now is the time to do it. Go ahead and complete any modifications before posting. You don't want to get caught in any conflicting messaging or expectations.

Where We Are So Far

At this point, you've done the work to clarify the job function, finalize the job description (initial and updates), collect competitive market data, and complete a pay assessment – where you reviewed internal and external levels to understand targeted levels of pay for both affordability and equity. You now have a compensation philosophy, and you feel good that your range for presenting offers is aligned with your organizational goals and values.

Now, it's time to put yourself out there and see what you attract.

If you have an internal recruiter or are utilizing an external agency to help you pursue talent, the due diligence you just completed should be the talking points that they would share to inspire someone to want to join your organization.

Side note: If you wouldn't come to work for you, what can you do to change that? If it isn't pretty, now is the time to craft a compelling message and opportunity (or make some changes internally).

Concepts to Revisit

Make a list of compensable factors in your job description. What education and experience levels are you looking for? What are the working conditions your new hire will be expected to perform in? How much or how little supervision do you intend to give them?

💡 Pick five job descriptions that are similar to what you're looking for, ranging from the low end to the high end of the market pay spectrum. List out each of the following: base salary, variable pay, total target cash, and the core compensable factors provided in the data collected.

💡 Write your compensation philosophy.

💡 Does anything need to change about the job you previously defined? If so, now is the time to do it. Go ahead and complete any modifications before posting. You don't want to get caught in any conflicting messaging or expectations.

Chapter 4:
Attract

If you hire good people, give them good jobs, and pay them good wages, generally something good is going to happen.

- James Sinegal

Determine what behaviors and beliefs you value as a company, and have everyone live true to them. These behaviors and beliefs should be so essential to your core, that you don't even think of it as culture.

- Brittany Forsyth

Now that we've defined the job role, written a description, and done the market research, it's time to go to work attracting candidates.

Attracting the right talent is just like the act of selling. It is a difficult and often challenging process. So you may find that you'll have to do the hard work and define exactly why someone would want to work in the organization. Your first step before even posting your job description online is to create your Employee Value Proposition.

Employee Value Proposition

Your employee value proposition is a reflection of the value you bring to the employee in return for the value they bring to you. It shouldn't be a detailed description of your variable pay program, but it should allude to the idea of pay performance and what experience the individual will have in their success. It doesn't need to describe all your total rewards benefits, but it does need to show that you prioritize employee health, well-being, and other values that differentiate your organization. The emphasis should be on what's in it for them.

When crafting your employee value proposition, take into account your mission and purpose. However, you want to make the statement about the employee, not the employer.

For example, if I were hiring for a sales position for Sales Comp Guy, LLC., this would not be an employee value proposition:

Sales Comp Guy is looking for a go-getter salesperson to meet with prospective clients and close deals. This person should be a team player, have a good work ethic, and be a creative thinker.

On the other hand, here is an example of an employee value proposition.

Working for Sales Comp Guy provides you the opportunity to reach your fullest potential, making use of your creativity, drive, and ambition while being rewarded and recognized for that contribution.

Here are a few examples from other brands:

Nike: We aim to foster inclusion and embrace diversity throughout our business, teams and culture to bring us closer to the consumer, empower our employees to realize their full potential and create breakthrough innovations for athletes.[15]

Apple: This is where individual imaginations gather together, committing to the values that lead to great work. Here, you'll do more than join something — you'll add something.[16]

Harver: Our culture is driven by our people. From generous time off to Summer Friday hours and paid family leave, we want each Harverian to have the flexibility and freedom they need to bring their most authentic self to both work and home life.[17]

💡 Review your company values and really think about what you want for your new employee and how those connect to your Employee Value Proposition.

Your Current State of Affairs

Before you can begin to invite someone new into your organization, check in on the people who are already there. Your current employee engagement factors largely into your ability to attract new hires.

Go onto your organization's social media sites and observe any engagement, negative or positive, from your current employees. Check out your reviews on Glassdoor. Maybe you see that they're really loving their jobs and sharing that love with their own social followings. Maybe they've got nothing good to say. Maybe they aren't participating at all.

You'll know if you see anything that requires immediate attention. An employee having a bad day once in a while is normal. However, if there appears to be a mutiny forming, you'll need to address any systemic issues before you can grow.

On the other hand, if there seems to be a positive attitude all around, it's a good idea to take some actions to improve engagement. How ever your team bonds, whether it be office birthday parties or participating in a charity 5k together, be sure to include those things on your social media so that prospective new hires can get a feel for what life is like working for your organization.

Important note: don't create engagement activities just for the appearance of a healthy culture on social media.

These things need to be authentic to who you are as an organization. If you and your team aren't the fun and games types, don't try to do things that aren't enjoyable for you. Dinner can be sufficient. Lunch out can be enough. Keep in mind that even the little things can make a big difference. Maybe you bought a new coffee machine for the office or celebrated some workiversaries this week. Keep it simple. Keep it real. No need to create solutions where there are no problems.

This brings us to the different types of recruiting.

Two Types of Recruiting

Active recruiting means going to where the candidates are and approaching them more directly. Passive recruiting means announcing you have a job opening and waiting for the candidates to show up.

Those are the simple definitions, but for the rest of this chapter, we'll talk about different forms of passive and active recruiting. While it may seem like one form is better than another, in reality, it's important to find the right balance for your organization and the talent acquisition strategy that can have the most effective short-term results and long-term success.

Active Recruiting

1. Outreach tools like LinkedIn, Phenom, Monster, Indeed, etc. allow you to locate and reach out to candidates whose resumés match your job description. You can invite them to apply or contact you directly.

   These tools are an excellent way to find talent on a budget and to market your brand as an employer. According to LinkedIn, small businesses spend between $3k-$5k to find the right person for the job.[18] Taking advantage of online outreach tools can help alleviate some of that cost by prequalifying candidates using stored resumés and allowing you to consolidate your hiring tools to save money.

2. Show up at local labor markets, career fairs, conferences, and networking events. In spite of world events and the rise of online outreach tools, face-to-face networking and recruiting are still going strong. Showing up at fairs and conferences allows candidates to not only meet you but also ask any questions they may have about your organization, get a feel for the culture, and apply on the spot. People like to work with people they like, know, and

trust. It's just like how consumers prefer to buy from people they like, know, and trust.

3. Referral programs are arguably the best means small businesses have for recruiting new hires. Your employees and past employees (assuming they left on good terms) are excellent sources for generating candidate leads. Most individuals want to be helpful, and even more so if there's a financial reward in store for them.

   Sometimes, you're hiring their new boss. One twist on the referral program is giving them the ability to cast a vote for their manager. Invite employees to recommend a new employee—either internally or externally. Not only will you get referrals, but they'll be empowered by having a say in who's going to be their next leader.

A little more about referral programs.

If you don't already have a referral program, consider one of the following ideas:

Offer a financial bonus with milestone payouts. There's always the risk that a new hire won't work out, so you don't want to shell out bonuses upon hiring only to find you're going to have to do it all over again with a new candidate. Consider offering the cash after a probationary period (like 60 or 90 days).

Want to encourage more interaction with your company from potential referrals? Throw a hiring mix-and-mingle. Provide food and beverages—everyone appreciates that—and invite your employees to bring anyone they think may be interested in working with you. This is a fun way to get to know people in a casual, friendly environment.

Passive Recruiting

1. Your website's "career" page is an extremely valuable resource. Look back at the examples given under the employee value proposition section of this chapter. Each of those examples was found on that company's careers page. I encourage you to check out the pages for ideas for your own career page.

   Keep in mind that this page should be mostly about your prospective hire and what's in it for them. It should also include valuable information about your organization, but keep the details trimmed down to things you think will most interest your prospects. Remember that there is still an About Us section on your website for those who want to move about the company and its leadership. It's just that this section is all about them and why you.

2. Social media presence matters. Whether you like it or not, your social media presence is (or should be) a reflection of who you are as an organization. Post regularly, be authentic, and keep it simple. Prospective candidates are highly likely to research you via social media, but they don't need a lot of technical information or job descriptions. They're primarily looking to see if they would be a good fit culturally.

3. Create a talent network or funnel. Maybe you're not quite ready to actively recruit, or maybe you know there will be some jobs coming up in the future. Creating a talent network helps you maintain relationships with potential prospects who've shown interest in your organization and whose skills and values match what you're likely to be looking for.

Just like sales, having a long-term mentality about talent is important for your success in attracting the right person. The right person for your organization will likely take longer than you expected. And the first person that you come across may not be the best fit. It's an ongoing process, and the awareness of that process is important to gain perspective and patience for the journey.

A little more about networking and relationship management.

This isn't a one-time project and requires long-term nurturing. You'll need to regularly assess and update your relationships with passive candidates who possess the competencies you think will align with your organization's future needs.

So, what is a "talent network??" Essentially, it's a list of people you've met through social media, job fairs, referrals, etc. These people are not currently looking for jobs, or they are not who you're presenting looking at to fill the current positions. Ideally, you've had some sort of contact with them and identified them as somebody you're interested in working with one day when the right position and timing align.

Your LinkedIn network might be a great place to stay connected with this list. Perhaps you prefer email. Regardless, you want to nurture that list, keep them engaged, and ultimately hire directly from this group in the future.

Engaging your list is a fine balance between offering value and not being too overbearing in your communication. You're keeping the relationship alive without asking anything of it until the day you ask for applications.

Once you do decide to hire someone, it's important to remember that they haven't exited the network; they've just entered a new phase. Keep that long-term mindset, and you can still nurture that talent by providing career development opportunities and watching out for leadership skills that you may want to promote.

Like any aspect of life—not just recruiting—always surround yourself with quality people. You will eventually find the opportunity to support each other. If you have this perspective in mind, you will do good by them, and they will do good by you. It may be that you never have quite the right need to employ them, but it's also very possible that these same people refer a customer to you 10 years down the road because of your kindness and relationship.

Pitfalls of the Process

Attracting employees can take time, and it can be a frustrating process. There are plenty of pitfalls to avoid as well. Watch out for these potential setbacks:

- Misrepresentation: Social media is great, but it's also a place where you can be anyone you want to be or look like anyone you want to be. Just because they can 'talk the talk' and have the profile picture to prove it doesn't mean they can walk the walk. The same goes for you and your organization. Be real. Be authentic.

- Attracting the wrong people: If the candidates who are approaching you seem way off base from what you're looking for, you may not be presenting your organization or your job offer accurately. Go back and look through the job description and posting you created to make sure it's right. Be sure to check your website as well.

- Temptation to Lowball: It's always tempting to grab a good deal. But when it comes to hiring someone, you need to make the right offer for the candidate. If they know their worth and you lowball them, they'll walk. If they don't yet know their worth and you lowball them, eventually, it will catch up with you.

- Settling: Even in the best of markets, matching up with the right candidate can be time-consuming and frustrating. Be patient and put in the time. **The cost of hiring a sales replacement is far greater than the cost of waiting for the right one**.

- Bias: Be careful about how you accept or reject a resumé. Unconscious bias can easily creep in. Give yourself a pep talk before browsing candidate information to remind yourself to be objective and look at the experience provided in each resumé. The same is true for confirmation bias – you end up seeing exactly what you want to see. Be sure to be open to alternatives and variances from your initial thoughts, especially when reading resumés and overcoming first impressions.

As an example, in my personal experiences of hiring, I have had times when I interviewed for a position, and as we spoke, I was crafting new conceptual positions for them. These positions were how I could see their talents be most effective. These temporary deviations didn't help me focus on executing the immediate job I had, but they did help keep individuals in a talent pool for new jobs that may arise. As I can see how various people can be successful in the organization, I had to stop and consciously pull back and recognize that the immediate task at hand is filling the current job. It is always a good reminder of the value of doing the pre-work because if the scope of the job is too open-ended, it is very difficult to align the right person with the current business needs and performance levels desired.

Essentially, attracting an employee is about selling your organization. If you create the right messaging around who you are as an organization and what the role entails, you should attract the attention of the right candidates.

Although there will be highs and lows in the process, in the end, you'll meet the right person for the job.

Chapter 5:
Screening and Interviewing

I don't focus on what I'm up against. I focus on my goals and I try to ignore the rest.

- Venus Williams

Our goals can only be reached through a vehicle of a plan, in which we must fervently believe, and upon which we must vigorously act. There is no other route to success.

- Pablo Picasso

As the world continues to be more connected, we find ourselves with access to a more diverse array of resources than ever before. One U.S. organization, realizing some of its roles could be done remotely, decided to open its job postings to international candidates. The hiring team went through all of their usual processes for vetting and selecting a candidate and was pleased to make an offer to an up-and-coming salesperson from Germany.

The onboarding and ramp-up went well, and the new hire quickly became adept at his job. However, after almost two years, the organization reassessed its sales strategy and determined that this new role no longer supported its business direction. As they didn't have room to move the new hire to another position, they put together a generous severance package and had an uncomfortable conversation with him.

It seemed to go well, but a few days later, the company was contacted by the former employee's lawyer. As it turned out, the U.S. organization's idea of a "generous severance package" didn't match what the German employee was entitled to according to his country's worker protection laws. Furthermore, the lawyer was alleging that the cause for the firing was illegal.

Now, the organization is no longer out of the cost of a severance package; they also have to retain the council and potentially make amends for any inadvertent wrongdoings on their part. The financial costs were devastating, and the damage to the organization's reputation will likely cost them in the long term.

I'm sharing this story to bring home the gravity of what you're about to do when you move forward with the hiring process. Hopefully, your attempts to attract prospective new hires have resulted in a stack of resumés. But now the serious work begins.

Before getting into the logistics of this process, let's talk about how vitally important it is to put the time and effort into getting this right. You're probably aware that the cost of retaining an employee is far less than the cost of hiring a new one, so you understand the value of having employees that you want to keep around.

Additionally, the costs of recuperating from a bad hire can be more extreme than you might think. Hiring the wrong candidate can result in a poor cultural fit, an employee with a skills or experience gap, internal or external customer misalignments, and some rather high costs. Keep these things in mind:

- You can't always just fire someone if you get it wrong. While most states in the U.S. have "at-will" work laws where employers can terminate for many non-illegal reasons, many countries have stricter requirements for dismissing an employee.

- Severance might be mandated. In some countries, such as Canada, Australia, and the UK, severance mandates require the employer to pay severance once a particular criterion is met. Many others have notice periods as well.

- You may be stuck with this hire for longer than you'd like. This can happen because of the two points above or simply because the cost of firing and rehiring is prohibitive.

With the stakes so high, it is essential to spend this time getting all your ducks in a row before you begin speaking to candidates for your role. Not only does planning out the process help streamline your hiring activities, but it also helps protect you in the event that something goes wrong.

Compliance Measures

To keep yourself and your organization covered, as well as to provide a fair interview experience for prospective candidates, there are a few things that need to be researched. If you've already got this covered, feel free to skip ahead. Otherwise, make sure you are compliant in all of the following areas:

1. Understand Federal, State, and Local Labor Laws and Regulatory Expectations

2. Pay Transparency Requirements

3. Equity and Anti-Discrimination Laws

4. Background Checks and Privacy Policies

5. Immigration and Work Authorization

6. Employment Contracts Requirements

7. Interview and Onboarding Process Consistency

8. Health and Safety Regulations

9. OSSCP (Organizational Security and Cybersecurity Policy) Requirements

10. Recordkeeping and Documentation Practices

11. Employee Classification Adherence

12. Diversity and Inclusion Policies

In the US, there are other regulations from organizations like the Office of Federal Contract Compliance Programs (OFCCP) and the Equal Employment Opportunity Commission (EEOC) that your organization may also have to adhere to. Now that we've talked about what's at stake and covered compliance let's outline the hiring process.

Outlining the Process

There are so many advantages to documenting a process, and if your organization already has one, you don't need to read this part. However, if you don't, then taking the time to create a process so that you can create a consistent experience for all candidates, as well as your hiring leaders, will help prevent discrepancies and make hiring a little easier. You'll need to know:

- The number of interviews needed before a decision is handed out

- The medium or style of interview (phone, video, in-person)

- Who will be involved in each of the interviews

- The cadence and length of the interviews

- The process for the interview team - to include feedback collection

- Established expectations of interviewees at each step of the interview process

Once you have these things in place, you can start working on the elements and flow of the interview. You may want to follow something similar to the following:

- Start with introductions, where applicable

- Next, clarify the job to ensure understanding and alignment

- Begin with your questions

- Invite them to ask their questions

- Clarify the next steps and timing

If your interview requires a presentation or other demonstration of technical knowledge and skillset, the flow may vary from the outline illustrated above.

Reviewing Resumés

You've got a stack of resumés in front of you. A moment ago, that stack looked like an endless possibility. Now, it looks like drudgery. It can be tempting to mindlessly skim through and glance at keywords. Or maybe even pass the task off to someone else. However, this part of the screening process is crucial and deserves to be approached with focus and intention.

Doing a proper review will lay the groundwork for a smooth interview process. Or it might reveal that you're not attracting the right prospective employees and you won't be interviewing anytime soon. If the latter is the case, go back to your job description and job posting and review it for potential issues that might be inadvertently misleading applicants.

It's worth noting that the costs of not carefully reviewing applications include time and energy wasted on interviewing the wrong potential employees or the reverse—missing out on the right ones.

Quick Tips

- Know what you're looking for and what you're looking to avoid.

- Review applications and resumés as quickly as possible.

- Follow an organized review system for consistency. The real benefit is speed and accuracy of alignment with expectations.

- Look for reasons to reject the resumé.

- Sort into three piles: yes, no, and maybe.

- Be consistent to avoid bias.

If you've created your interview questions, you likely already have a good idea of what you're looking for. Now you're going to switch gears. Rather than looking for the things you like, you're going to look for reasons to reject a resumé.

Create a rubric for yourself to keep consistent as you review the resumés. Prioritize the must-haves or non-negotiables. If you're dead set on finding someone with five years of experience in sales and a bachelor's degree, your list might look like this:

- ☐ 5+ years of experience in sales

- ☐ Demonstrated success in exceeding quota

- ☐ Bachelor's degree

- ☐ Comfort in managing long and complex sales processes

- ☐ Proven track record of closing business similar to yours

- ☐ Industry and market segment experience

Your list may look difference. Maybe you don't need them to have industry experience, but it would be nice. If it's not a reason to say no, don't put it on the list. If you're hiring for entry-level, you likely won't need to see evidence of advancement or promotion, but you might like to see evidence of personal or professional development or ambition.

💡 *Make your list of non-negotiables, must-haves, and "like to haves."*

The point of this exercise is to identify your hard requirements and formulate a review system you can follow. This will help you move through your stack of applications faster, and it will also help prevent any biased judgments. Remember, this list should align with the wording of your job description and job posting. If not, you may need to go back and modify any shift in expectation.

A note on bias: The review system you create can be helpful in preventing unconscious bias. One good example is the idea of a consecutive sequence of experience in the resumé. Let's say that you've decided gaps in experience are a "hard no" for you when reviewing. Now, say you are looking through a resumé with a lot of promising items like industry experience, a long list of attractive accomplishments, and an exceptionally high-quality education—but there are big, unexplainable gaps. You may be tempted to move that resumé forward at that moment because you got dazzled by the other qualities.

Now, let's say you've moved on, forgotten about that little exception to your rule, and you run across another good resumé with many dazzling accomplishments and experiences. This time, there's a two-year gap that's accounted for under the heading "caregiver: July 2020-September 2022." It's not a far-fetched guess to assume that this application comes from a woman who chose to stay home and take care of a child or an elderly parent for a couple of years. Whatever the case, you have inadvertently created a conflict that was not necessary, to begin with.

Now you have a dilemma. I won't get into the different decisions you might make; the point of this example is to show that had you stuck to your "reasons to say no" list, you wouldn't have to face this decision in the first place.

All decisions and processes you establish before diving into your stack of resumés will help you avoid blockers, inconsistencies, and wasted time and energy.

The screening Before the Interview

A friend of mine, I'll call him Bryan for the purposes of this book, had an incredibly unique experience with the consequences of not doing your due diligence in the pre-screening phase. There was a prospective hire, and we'll call him Todd, who was being pushed on Bryan's sales manager. The sales manager didn't feel he had much choice, but he gave Todd an interview. There were some red flags that prompted the manager to go to his boss and request some clarity. The boss insisted that he really liked Todd. Todd was a standup guy and would be a good hire. So, the manager hired him.

The organization hosted a big annual training event, and Bryan went, expecting the usual conversations with colleagues and sit-downs with higher-ups. The event was business casual, and everyone came presenting their best. When Todd entered the room, everyone was surprised to see him looking disheveled and, strangely, sporting a tire track down the middle of his shirt. When asked, he claimed his bag had been dropped and his shirt run over at the airport.

On top of his strange presentation, he also made a terrible impression in front of the CEO, using coarse language and just generally behaving inappropriately. Bryan reached out to his manager to share the disturbing news, and the sales manager reached out to his boss, who finally agreed to send Todd to another territory, down in Texas.

Come to find out, as soon as Todd stepped off the plane in Texas, the police were there to arrest him for attempted murder.

The moral of this true story is - to do your own due diligence and always screen your candidate – in spite of what others insist.

Take your "yes" stack of applications and get ready to do even more preparation. First of all, this should be a very small stack. If not, you either have a really good problem on your hands, or you need to run them all through the review process one more time.

Once you have the stack you want to work with, it's time to do some pre-interview screening. You may have a recruiter to do much of this work, but it is important to recognize the process flow and experience that your prospective employee should be expecting.

If you're doing this part yourself, you'll want to make phone calls. You may choose to send an email prior to the call, but emails can be unreliable, and you definitely want to touch base via phone before inviting someone to an interview.

If you're uncomfortable with this outreach process, give yourself 1-2 minutes to create the initial call outline or simple script. The flow of this initial call should include pleasantries, sharing of backgrounds, and an outline of the role and the company, but don't spend a lot of time on it.

This call should be relatively short and no more than thirty minutes. Remember, they should be waiting to hear from you, but expect to leave a voicemail, so be clear on what you want them to respond with - curiosity, availability, comfort, and understanding of the job, etc. The phone conversation is to validate that they can carry on a conversation like you'd need them to do with a client or prospect. Remember that this is all before the interview. You are confirming that they still have an interest and collecting some perspective on soft skills prior to the technical questions. This is also where you can outline the job, ask a few easy questions, and gain some behavioral insights.

Be sure to understand that these conversations go both ways – leave time for questions in both directions.

The first question might be the tried-and-true, "Tell me about yourself." Unless this is your candidate's first interview, they'll be prepared for an open-ended question like this. If they happen to have time for that first conversation, utilize it.

Be prepared. It gives you an opportunity to hear how they speak, learn a little about how they see themselves, and gain insight into their communication skills.

After that, cater your questions to any specific concerns you may have about their fit in the position.

- *I see you previously worked for an engineering firm; what makes you interested in moving into the healthcare sector?*

- *What was it like transitioning from inside to outside sales?*

- *What attracted you to our job posting?*

Just like during the application review process, your goal here is to find reasons to eliminate this prospective candidate. You should be looking for red flags or anything that tells you the intended person is a poor fit for your role. And likewise, let them cross you off their list. It goes both ways.

As you approach the end of the call, remember your defined process and consider a prompt for bringing it to a close. Don't make any promises. Even if you're very excited about the candidate, focus on sharing the process and timing. Set reasonable expectations for what is happening next. Try something like:

- *We'll be in touch soon, one way or the other.*

- *Enjoyed the conversation. You can expect an email from us in no more than three days.*

- *I'll give you a call if we decide to set up an interview. Otherwise, I will email you.*

- *We've got a few other candidates to talk to, but you should hear something by next Monday.*

Remember, job hunters are often under a great deal of stress. Anything you can do to make the future less uncertain is helpful. Letting them know what to expect in terms of future conversations and then following through with your promises is just good form. Clearly define the next steps of the process.

💡 *Write your screening phone call script and process for quick and easy reference.*

A note on social media: After the call, it's a good idea to take a look at your prospect's public social media accounts. You may think it better to do this before the call, but I recommend it after. Not everything you see on social media falls into the category of "good" or "bad." You will not want distractions or personal judgments fogging the initial interaction.

After the call, you'll have some context or lens through which to view social media besides your own first impressions. You do want to validate that they know how to be professional and manage their public image.

While you want to look at all major social channels, LinkedIn is particularly important. A lack of presence on this or other social media channels isn't necessarily a red flag, but if they have a presence, you'll want to cross-reference what you see there with what you've learned from their resumé and your initial phone call. There are mixed feelings on this topic, but the way they show up in the public forum matters, especially for sales positions.

The Interview

At last, you've found your top three to five promising candidates, you've set up appointments, and you're ready to interview. You've already prepared your questions before you start sifting through resumés. Now, let's talk about what happens in the interview room.

You first have to decide whether the interview is going to be in person or virtual. It may go without saying that it is important to supply accommodations for interviewees who may be currently living at a distance from your organization.

Then, you have to decide whether it's going to be a one-on-one interview or a panel interview.

During the interview, you're going to explain the role and responsibilities along with how they are tied to the success of the organization. You want to paint a picture of what a day in the life of this role looks like, as well as how they affect the broader goals of the entire organization.

Get into detail about the sales process, including the market, prospects, the customer journey, the length of the sales cycle, and the way sales are rewarded (no need to get into the details of pay right now). Ensure they have clarity regarding their functional responsibilities. Ask the interviewee how they feel about the process and if they have any questions.

If compensation comes up, you can certainly share, but it's also important to really gauge what level of compensation they are looking for or if there are any compensation obstacles that need to be overcome. Get comfortable with wording that works for you to assess their expectations.

Your Interview Questions

Next, begin asking your behavioral questions. You don't need to ask specifically about accomplishments or responsibilities included in the resumé; that's what references are for. Keep your questions open-ended and watch for red flags as well as potential opportunities.

The more you interview, the more you learn about the best ways to interview. Throughout this process, consider taking notes about the questions you're asking and why you're asking them. Eventually, you can create a company interviewing guide to ensure consistency throughout your organization.

The subject of interview questions may seem obvious. You can find all kinds of good (and bad) advice on the Internet. But the truth is, you have to be purposeful about how you approach this process. Your questions matter because you most likely won't find a resumé that precisely matches your job description. Your goal is to find a candidate who has the commensurate experience and behaviors to fulfill the responsibilities of your role.

Using behavioral interview questions is currently the most effective technique for predicting the future performance of a potential employee.[19] These questions are designed to help you measure the unmeasurable. You don't need behavioral questions on objective skills that can be tested—operating equipment, building a spreadsheet, and public speaking are all skills you can see for yourself. But there are many skills that can't be tested. Leading a cross-functional team, closing a difficult sale, and consistently meeting deadlines are all examples of skills that can only be discovered through behavioral interview questions.

Quick Tips

- Think about the soft skills you'll be looking for during the interview.

- List your top five priority skills that can't be tested or measured.

- Avoid using "Yes" or "No" questions.

- Create questions that engage the interviewee and promote thought rather than lead them to the answer you want to hear.

A good behavioral question involves an open-ended prompt designed to get the prospect talking about their experience. You'll be looking for evidence of behaviors that are needed in your job role, as well as the prospect's ability to communicate effectively and leverage their skills in a variety of scenarios.

Start your question with a lead-in centering on a job scenario or challenge that your prospect will likely encounter. Open it up for them to describe a time when they exhibited the behavior that is transferrable to your role. You may want to hear about how they managed their time, how they evolved the customer relationship, or how they

persuaded and influenced a prospective customer to an optimal outcome.

I recently interviewed a few sales leaders to find
out what their favorite interview questions are.
Here are a few:

1. How would you approach a short sales cycle
   differently than a long sales cycle?

   • Short cycles call for reps that can close
     quickly, and long sales cycles require a
     much more careful, tailored approach.
     They're drastically different, and your
     candidate should recognize this, both
     psychologically and programmatically.
     A good follow-up is "How did you stay
     organized?" or "How did you manage the
     process differently?".

2. When do you stop pursuing a client?

   • The right answer here will depend on
     your company's process, but in general,
     the more tenacious and persistent a rep
     is willing to be, the better. Trish Bertuzzi,
     the founder of The Bridge Group, recom-
     mends six to eight attempts before throw-
     ing in the towel. Personally, I'd advocate

that the correct answer is "never". It's not, no, just not now.

3. How do you keep a smile on your face during a hard day?

    •   Appraise the person's attitude towards rejection. Do they need time to shake off an unpleasant conversation? Or do they bounce back immediately? See which strategies they use to recover and move on. Acknowledging how they manage stress and frustration or if they have structures of emotional support in place, as these outlets are paramount to their individual success.

4. Have you ever turned business away? If so, why?

    •   Selling to everyone and anyone — even if a salesperson knows it's not in the prospect's best interest — is a recipe for disaster. Make sure your candidate is comfortable with turning business away if the potential customer isn't a good fit. This is a good test of ethics and integrity. It's an excellent place to gauge alignment with the culture and values of the organization.

For a comprehensive list of questions, view the appendix.

In each of these examples, we start with an aspect of a job the prospect is likely to encounter. Then, we prompt them to describe an action (management, organization, approaching/communicating). You want to hear a story of their experience and how they responded, especially during a challenging time or experience.

If your prospect doesn't have any direct experience with the behaviors you're asking about, consider prompting them with a role-play question.

- *Your prospective customer has requested five meetings with you, keeping you in conversation about the sale but continually evading financing the deal. Talk to me about how you would handle that.*

- *You have ten clients in various stages of your pipeline. Describe how you move them each further along the buyer's journey at the various stages.*

- *You're given a list of phone numbers from a marketing conference. How do you start?*

Ideally, it's better if the prospect has experience, but depending on your job description and budget, you may have to compromise. Role-playing the scenarios will still give you the needed insight into how your prospect thinks, adapts, and communicates, especially during periods of ambiguity and stress.

A note on leadership traits: Even if you're hiring for an entry-level position, you want to watch for leadership skills. At their most basic, leadership skills can include self-discipline, taking ownership of your role, collaborating with others, motivating others, coordinating external stakeholders to a common vision and outcome, knowing how to ask empowering questions, and enlisting others to achieve a goal.

As you move up the organizational hierarchy, you'll see these traits develop into the ability to form a team, influence and empower other individuals, bring out leadership skills in others, make good decisions and judgments on how to manage projects, and more.

Ideally, you'll see evidence of these traits in the interview process. Try to include at least one prompt specifically geared toward revealing leadership behaviors.

Of course, not everyone you hire needs or wants to "climb the ladder" into a leadership position, but they do need to have the skills to take the lead in their own roles and contribute to your organization above and beyond the role requirements. It may not be leadership from a managerial perspective, but sales must be proficient in "leading from the side" without any formal organizational power. They must be successful at exercising those leadership qualities in the prospective account or client in order to secure business and maintain successful relationships.

Candidate Questions

Next, it's time to open the floor for questions from your prospective candidate. Since this is a sales job, they may very quickly get into the topic of how they earn commission or incentive pay. If this is a new role, it'll be far tougher to address that. If it is an existing role, you at least have some history to share. But that's why we did some prep work to know what we could afford to offer. Be prepared to field questions like:

- Can you describe your company culture?

- What's your remote work policy?

- Can you give me an idea of the target earnings for the position?

- What does the quota look like?

- Do you offer any career development opportunities?

- How will you measure success for me in my role?

There's no predicting what you'll be asked, but job seekers use the same Google you do, so it might pay to do a search of "questions to ask potential employers." Chances are your interviewee has done the same search and will come up with some of the questions they've found that way.

💡 *Thinking about how to reveal important information about your prospective hire, craft some interview questions that will show whether this person has the behaviors you're looking for in a candidate.*

It has been said that the greatest skill needed by a salesperson is to ask good questions and be an active and engaged listener. While I believe that to be true, I believe that **being genuinely curious and interested in the other person** in the conversation is paramount to long-term sales success.

Other Things to Observe in the Interview

Again, if you've done this before, you may be familiar with a lot of what I'm about to share. However, many hiring managers are so focused on the resumé that they forget to investigate aspects like:

- Does the candidate have the ability to carry on a conversation?

- Do they show interest or excitement in the job/opportunity?

- How comfortable are they at asking engaging and/or challenging questions?

- Did they seem like they were listening or just waiting for you to stop talking?

- Would a client want to spend time with them?

Finally, just like in the initial screening phone call, have a plan ready for wrapping up the interview. You don't want to make any promises; just indicate that you'll be in touch once you've finished the other interviews. It's nice to give an idea of when that will be and let them know that they can expect a message or response one way or another. Speak to your process, and don't be afraid to overcommunicate.

Watch Out for These Interview Pitfalls

If you've done all the up-front prep work when sifting through resumés and documenting a process, the interview should go pretty well. But there is always potential for challenges. Here are a few potential pitfalls to avoid during an interview:

- Don't bring in your bias if you have previous knowledge of an applicant. The past is the past. Just because they might have been a jerk in high school doesn't mean they haven't grown up and become self-aware and conscientious adult.

- Be careful not to simply favor an applicant based on shared interests or views on things like sports, movies, music, etc.

- Watch out for unconscious bias, such as associating certain work characteristics with a particular age, race, or gender.

- Purge the "stereotypes" of a good candidate. People come in all shapes and sizes with a wide variety of haircuts and fashion choices, along with makeup and jewelry. Open your mind to the possibility of value in all forms.

- Don't let your own fatigue influence your decision. If you're too tired to choose, take some time to rest and reflect (or restart the process).

- Don't make up your mind right at the beginning. Make sure to take in all the information provided throughout the interview.

The reality is that there is always high demand for good talent, and there is nothing about the process that is easy, and the employer no longer has leverage over employees. You want to view the experience as a mutually beneficial relationship or partnership—especially in a sales hire.

The name of the game is purpose and intent. If you follow these steps in screening candidates, and you do it with an open mind and intentionality, you should end up with either the best possible candidate or the conclusion that you need to keep looking.

Sometimes, it is appropriate to wait. Simply making a decision on what's in front of you isn't always the best decision. I have provided a number of favorite sales interview questions that have been shared with me over the years. Remember to review Appendix A for the full list.

Concepts to Revisit

💡 *Thinking about how to show important information about your prospective hire, craft some interview questions that will show whether this person has the behaviors you're looking for in a candidate.*

💡 *Write your phone screening script and interview outline, as well as timelines. Have them handy for quick reference or reminder.*

💡 *Document your process so you can manage it. It should include interview questions, timing expectations, process and number of interviews, FAQs, description of the role, and scripts if you need to rely on them.*

💡 *Ask about pay challenges, objectives, or issues that need to be overcome based on what they know. Be sure to inquire about their expectations on compensation.*

Chapter 6:
The Offer

*If you don't know where you are going,
you'll end up someplace else.*

-Yogi Berra

*If you can't describe what you are doing
as a process, you don't know what
you're doing.*

- W. Edwards Deming

Maybe these comments presume you don't already have a clear, documented, and regularly used process for making an offer. If you do, you don't need to spend much time on this section. Additionally, if you have a full-time recruiter, your role in this process may vary. The takeaways of this chapter are intended to ensure a smooth workflow and the salient points of the engagement with prospective employees.

With the interview process concluded, you are now in one of several situations. Maybe you found no qualified talent for your open position. In this case, wash, rinse, and repeat—go back to the beginning, make any tweaks you deem necessary to your role description and screening strategy, and then try again. You absolutely should not settle for someone who isn't right for the position just for the sake of filling a position.

You may find yourself in the scenario of having one outstanding qualified candidate. Or you may find yourself with a couple of options. The rest of this chapter will address how to handle each of those scenarios.

How to Decline

Before moving into offer development, let's discuss declining. During the resumé screening, a simple form rejection is fine. But once you've been face-to-face with someone in an interview, the only truly respectful way to decline is over the phone. You are never too busy to be a good human being. People appreciate the respect provided to them.

Timing depends on a couple of considerations. If you know for sure that you won't be hiring this individual, then decline them immediately. Keep in mind that they are looking for work, possibly urgently, and having made it through the interview, they're likely on the edge of their seats waiting for an answer.

On the other hand, if you have a candidate who is in close second place, it's okay to wait on declining until after your first offer is accepted or declined the initial offer. However, once you've entered an agreement with the other candidate, it's time to decline that second candidate.

Quick Tips for Declining a Second-Place Candidate

- Start with a phone conversation. Let them know that while they were qualified, you ultimately had to go with another candidate.

- See if they are open to staying in touch.20 Be candid about your interest in them for potential future openings, and ask if they're interested in hearing from you in the future.

- Follow up consistently without leading them on. This is an essential part of keeping a talent pipeline. Follow-up every few weeks with check-in emails, company newsletters, or perhaps an invitation to a company open-house event. Be honest and clear about your lack of job openings, especially if you don't see anything opening up in the future. If your organization has opportunities regularly, then more frequent engagement is appropriate.

- Connect via LinkedIn to remain top-of-mind with the candidate should they be looking for work in the future.

- Remember, these are quality candidates that you would hire if you had a second opening. You want to stay in touch.

Creating the Offer

First, you want to create your package. You should already have a pay range and variable pay program from which to draw. As a reminder, when deciding on the total pay package, be sure you have already addressed:

- How much can I afford to offer?

- How competitive with the market is it?

- How does it compare to internal peers?

- What is the cost of training and ramp-up time?

- What percentage of pay-at-risk do I want to include?

- How can I make this offer attractive enough to get an immediate yes?

- How does this compare to any competitive offers in play or objections communicated?

- What's my plan in the event of a counteroffer?

You'll want to keep in mind that if you aren't recruiting in a state with pay transparency laws, your offer may be your candidate's first formal exposure to your compensation package. They likely have a desired amount. And you probably don't know that piece of information. So, it's a good idea to leave a little room for bargaining. Remember you are hiring for a sales role. Always expect some negotiation. In fact, it's unusual if they don't.

Note: You should have already collected some ranges of pay or historical performance levels from the conversation. Keep those in mind when messaging the verbal offer.

You also want to present an offer that illustrates what you feel about this candidate's potential value in the organization. If your offer is in the low range of market value for the role, during your offer conversation, you may want to lead in with a brief background and status of your company to help set the expectation. It's important to set any potential conflict on the table early, like your current budget limitations.

A note on internal equity: Take a look at other similar roles within your organization. Take note of the years of experience and levels of pay of the people in those roles. Compare their contributions and education with your candidate's and try to place that candidate in a fair position in terms of base pay and total target cash when establishing an offer. You don't necessarily want to hire someone with only five years of experience at a total target cash higher than someone else performing a similar role with over ten years of experience. If you are compelled to push higher, what's your plan to fill the gap for the incumbent?

Once you decide on a base salary and variable pay amount, make sure to clearly articulate the actions needed and outcomes desired in order to be successful in the role and how they can make the maximum amount possible under the variable pay plan.

Next, describe the benefits, including any healthcare coverage that will be provided along with your paid leave policy. Career development opportunities are often a priority for new hires—they want to know how they can grow within your organization. Describe any other perks included in the offer. This is where you highlight what makes you different culturally and if you have social or philanthropic programs as well.

You'll also want to consider what expenses will be paid, especially if you're hiring a field sales representative who will be doing a lot of traveling.

Explain any non-compete or non-disclosure agreements you'll require from them.

And lastly, include the starting date.

Because you want to be able to deliver that offer letter very quickly following that verbal offer, it is helpful to have that completed (or at least drafted) ahead of the conversation.

Your offer letter should include the following elements:

- A greeting and extension of the offer

- Information about the job, including job title, immediate supervisor, and job description (which can be attached)

- Explanation of the base and variable pay

- Explanation of the process for earning variable pay (simple demonstration of assignment and/or coverage if you have a formal sales incentive plan to follow)

- Essential benefits like health care, disability, time-off, 401-K, etc.

- Additional benefits and perks

- Information on allowances or expenses paid, especially if they are expected to be out of pocket or upfront

- Contractual agreements (non-solicit, non-compete), where required

- An acceptance deadline

💡 *Using the information you've gathered so far, craft an offer letter to your ideal candidate. Don't forget to factor in market value and internal equity considerations before finalizing the prospective offer.*

Making the Call

Many employers pass this task off to someone else, but as the hiring manager, you want to be the one to make the verbal offer directly. Just like the decline, you want to do this as soon as possible, both for the sake of your candidate's stress and to gain an agreement before the candidate moves on.

Making the call yourself allows you to counter any potential misunderstandings or questions. No one knows the offer better than you, and presentation matters. Explaining the components of the offer in the right order and in the right way can mean the difference between an acceptance or a decline. Ideally, you would have already collected a vibe on any potential conflicts or opposition prior to this conversation.

When you call, have the offer components in front of you as an outline for the phone conversation, and then follow these steps:

- Start with the intention. For example, "I'm pleased to offer you the position of..."

- Remind them of the job requirements

- Explain the compensation and breakdown of base and variable pay

- Describe other benefits like health care, retirement, etc.

- Mention a preferred start date

- Provide a deadline for acceptance or decline

- If you're nervous, remember that this should be good and exciting news

A note on the deadline—if you're feeling particularly good about the candidate's energy around your offer, it's okay to ask for an answer on the phone. Don't pressure them to decide, but don't be afraid to ask. You can approach them with an open-ended question like: "We're really excited to start your onboarding. How are you feeling about this offer?"

If you can't read their reaction, you can also use other questions:

- Does this match your expectations?

- How does this stack up against other offers you are receiving?

- Are we in a good place to move forward together?

You'd like a yes, but give them the opportunity to think it over.

Regardless of how they answer, end the conversation by letting them know what the next steps are. You will be sending over a formal written offer, and they should be checking their email accordingly. You need a response within the specific timeframe.

Dealing with Pushback /Offer Negotiation

- Ideally, you've already addressed objections and conflicts (money, title, timing, etc). This isn't the best place to negotiate, but that may be out of your control.

- The best thing you can do is prepare for potential areas of concession (usually money and start date), but it may be things like time off/vacation, education reimbursement, or benefits they are leaving on the table.

- If you know you will be comfortable paying a sign-on bonus for an earlier start date, then configure your price and be ready to exercise it.

- Of course, all of this back and forth will require a new offer crafted, but that is the value of trying to resolve as many of these things as possible in the screening and during the interview(s).

Getting the Signature

One thing you can pass off is the creation and delivery of the offer letter. After the phone call (verbal offer), be sure to send out the letter as soon as possible. When it comes to getting an official signature, there are several options. You can go the old-fashioned route and mail the letter to get a physical signature, or you can go digital.

Remember that this offer should not be the first time they are reading about anything of significance. Neither of you want any surprises at this point. Don't leave any openings for any difficult conversations.

If you haven't invested in digital contract management software, it's easy enough to search online for reviews or ask around your network for what other people are using.

Some well-known and popular digital options include:

- <u>DocuSign</u>

- <u>Adobe Acrobat Sign</u>

- <u>Agiloft</u>

- <u>PandaDoc</u>

- <u>ContractWorks</u>

- <u>Gatekeeper</u>

Many of these systems include other functionality that you may or may not want. You may very well already have something, but it is worthwhile to have a digital retention strategy, as I am sure you have one for your customers.

💡 *If you don't already subscribe to an app or system for digital workflow and retention, do some research. The right program can help you track and maintain your employee agreements with automation. This is just a small way you can increase efficiency at a low cost.*

Once you've received a signed agreement, your search is over, but the work is just getting started. Most employers recognize the sometimes seemingly insurmountable challenge of finding and hiring the right person. It's costly, time-consuming, stressful, and can slow down the forward movement of your organization.

But, once you find the right person, you want to begin setting them up for success as quickly as possible. So far, we've put all of the emphasis on the attraction of talent. We are going to cover some of the aspects of retention and motivation. In the next chapter, we'll talk about your new hire's first ninety days.

Concepts to Revisit

💡 *Using the information you've gathered so far, craft an offer letter to your ideal candidate. Don't forget to factor in market value and internal equity when deciding on final offers.*

💡 *If you don't already subscribe to an app or system for digital documents, retention, and signatures, do some research. The right program can help you track and maintain your contracts with automation. This is just a small way you can increase efficiency at a low cost.*

💡 *Be sure to really understand what you are willing to pay or concede on with the offer so you can be prepared to counter as needed.*

Chapter 7:
Onboarding

I truly believe that onboarding is an art. Each new employee brings with them a potential to achieve and succeed.

- Sarah Wetzel

The only source of knowledge is experience

- Albert Einstein

Your onboarding process is going to be unique to your organization, but the framework will include components common to any onboarding experience. Things like paperwork, orientation, training, compliance, and team building are parts of every onboarding experience.

Much study has been done on how to create an ideal onboarding experience, as this time period is critical to the long-term success of your new hire. According to Gallup, employees who experienced an exceptional onboarding experience are nearly three times as likely to say they are happy with their jobs.[21] Since onboarding can make or break this new relationship, it is crucial to put thought and care into this process. It requires thought, care, and attention. Once your new hire has their bearings and is operating independently, you can step back. But until then, it's important to pay attention.

The first 90 days

In this section, we'll look at the traditional onboarding timeline of 90 days. It's critical to understand, however, that completing onboarding is just the beginning for the new hire in terms of getting established. Over time, training and teaching shifts to coaching and advising. In fact, a recent Gallup poll found that it takes a full 12 months before a new hire finally reaches their full performance potential in their new role.[22]

The Paperwork

Prior to the first day on the job, any background checks, drug testing, etc., should be completed.

Onboarding often begins the same day as an offer is signed. You'll likely have a variety of forms and agreements you'll need your new hire to read or sign, including government forms (like the I-9, W-2, or 1099 if you're in the U.S.), non-disclosures, non-solicits, non-competes, the employee handbook, an outline of benefits. Note: As of the writing of this book, the future of non-competes is still up in the air with recent legislation.[23]

They'll also need to fill out any forms regarding their benefits enrollments, retirement or pension participation, and insurance policies, although many of these will require walk-throughs during the next step of the onboarding process.

The orientation:

On their first day, whether in the office or remote, it's nice to have a welcome gift or swag bag of some sort. A t-shirt with your company's logo or a coffee mug are good ideas to get started and can help the new hire begin to feel like one of the team. A physical gift makes an impact.

If in the office, you'll likely give them a tour of your facilities along with introductions to the executives and organizational leaders. Of course, you'll show them to any office or desk space that belongs to them now. Over the course of the next week, it's a good idea to arrange meetings with each department head so they can begin to understand the operational workflow within the organization.

Note from an outsider's perspective:

If you've ever been the "new kid in school," you know how frustrating it can be when the people there assume you understand their culture or activities. Before bringing in your new hire, gather your existing employees together and explain to them that integrating a new team member is a proactive process for everyone in the company.

Encourage them to reach out individually to the new hire and invite them to lunch or a coffee break. If the first Friday of every month is Hawaiian Shirt Day, then make sure your new hire knows so they can participate if they want. If birthdays are a big deal in the office, again, make the new hire aware. Also, taking the time to walk through many of the operational aspects like internal access, training requirements, printer location, etc. Don't forget the little stuff. Make sure they feel welcome and wanted.

Much of this feels like common sense or overkill to even mention, but the intent is to recognize the need to take a step back and acknowledge the nuances of integrating a new person into an existing culture with the hopes of them aligning while also pushing and challenging the organization as any good salesperson should do.

💡 *Brainstorm ways you can help your new hire more easily integrate into your team and environment.*

The First 90 Days:

As you embark on the first ninety days with your new hire, training is going to be your priority. If your organization is heavily reliant on technology, as most places are, the first area to focus on is your technology, tools, CRM, processes, procedures, and compliance.

Management Systems: If your organization uses project management or workflow software, it is essential that your new hire learn how to navigate this system as soon as possible. Missing out on information or failing to properly record work activities can cause disruptions downstream. The sooner your new hire knows how to work within your chosen software, the sooner they can be seamlessly integrated into your workflows.

Timekeeping Software: Many organizations require time tracking even if employees are salaried. If you require timesheets, make sure your new hire understands how and why to do this.

HR Management: Even if all of your pay and benefits management happens in-house, you likely have access to user portals through your benefits providers and payroll admin. Make sure your new hire has all the information they need to find details on managing their benefits selections and changes.

Various other tools: Walk your new hire through all the tools they'll need to do their job, including the CRM, quoting and proposal tools, access to office applications and data, training materials, marketing collateral, etc.

💡 *Make a list of the most important things your new hire needs to learn within the first 90 days. Now, map out a calendar to address each of those elements.*

Sales training should begin early in the first ninety days. This includes tactical tasks, meetings, and activities as well as big, long-term projects that are worth attention and investment. Both are aspects of learning and exposure within this new environment. There is value in letting them know how their efforts help to grow the organization.

You want the ramp-up time to be as short as possible for your salesperson, but keep in mind that average ramp-up times are over three months, and it can take up to a year for an employee to reach their full performance potential.

Tips for a Welcoming Onboarding Experience

- Starting onboarding on a Monday can make for an overwhelming week. Be sure to keep that in mind when deciding on a start date.

- Take the time to plan a welcoming event.

- Start with a welcome swag bag. Ideally, this should also be provided for remote starters.

- Create a social atmosphere by bringing in donuts or catering breakfast or lunch on your new hire's first day so they can get to know their coworkers.

- If you have a newsletter or social media platform, include a brief introduction and a photo to share broadly and acknowledge their joining the organization.

Vision and Values: Before you send your salesperson out to interact with prospective customers, you want to make sure they are firmly rooted in the goals, values, and culture of your organization. This affects not only their ability to represent you out in the world but also the way they communicate and sell. **They are the first impression your customers have of your organization**; make sure it's a good one.

The Thing Being Sold: You probably remember the old hair club for men commercial—I'm not just the president. I'm also a client. There's a lot to be said about being a fan and user of your own product. Sometimes, that just isn't possible, but you do want the salesperson to have the experience and perspective of the user of the product when they are trying to persuade a purchase. To ensure alignment, spend some time demonstrating the value of your product or service. Their full buy-in will translate into passion and authenticity out in the field.

The Sales Process: Will your sales employee be managing the beginning, middle, or end of the sales process? Is there a clearly defined sales process? Will your salesperson be creating leads? Will they be developing and closing transactions alone or as part of a joint effort? Whatever your sales process looks like, time management and understanding deal development are key to success, so make sure your new hire gets well acquainted with it from start to finish. Are there existing criteria or milestone events that distinguish deal health or progression? Be sure to set appropriate procedures and regular cadences for review and coaching. If it's a long sales process and there are many prospects in the pipeline to nurture, you'll want to train them on the best ways to manage and organize their business development efforts.

Territory Plan: Clear management of a territory (geography, revenue line, or account assignment) is key. This is a business plan for your business. Whatever the expectations are for upkeep, be sure they are documented. Make sure the new hire understands the physical (or virtual) territory they'll be operating in. That may be complex or simple. Either way, it is vital to have clear rules of engagement for interactions with clients, prospects, internal teams, and peers.

Generally, this also means that an Ideal Customer Profile exists, both in terms of their demographics (size, geography, industry, etc.) and the key decision-makers at the organization. Having this profile outline provides insight into the unique identifiers of the customer that tend to translate to better customer outcomes, more profitable engagements, and long-term successful relationships.

Opportunity and Account Planning

You want to set expectations for the level and cadence of engagement, communication, documentation, definitions, needs, etc. That may be informal conversations or an explicit process of weekly pipeline reviews, relationship map updates, opportunity coaching, or forecast reporting calls.

Incentive Pay Plan: Throughout the training process, continue to help your new salesperson connect their efforts with their potential rewards. Make sure they understand at what point they've achieved any benchmarks required to unlock their commissions or bonuses. Make sure they know when they can expect to see that pay hit their bank account. Take the temperature of the room and check to see if they find the incentives motivating. Hopefully, this conversation has already taken place, but if it is the first time, be open about the challenges and actively coach them on the actions needed to be successful in the role.

Learning the Job & The Ride Along: You may prefer to keep your new hire in the passenger seat for a while, letting them experience the sales process alongside someone who's been doing it for a while. If you haven't hired salespeople before, or you have very few salespeople, you may benefit from doing some work to investigate the types of sales functions needed in your organization. Determining the definitions of success aids in the training and development of talent.

Brent Adamson and Matthew Dixon, in their book *The Challenger Sale*, identified a profile of a salesperson who had performed better than their peers over time. Their work involved isolating demonstrated behaviors and tendencies in their approach to the interaction with customers and/or prospects. The *Challenger* profile was the debaters in the sales population. They have tendencies to bring differing viewpoints to the conversation. They have a keen awareness of the organization's inner workings and, as the name suggests, challenge the customer or prospect, their peers, managers, and stakeholders. Their value is in their insight and assertiveness.

I share the details of this because it is important to know what you are "coaching to" as it relates to the preferred sales behaviors, actions, and, ultimately, the outcomes you want demonstrated.

The Training Wheels: When it's time to turn your new hire loose, don't send them out to your hottest, most high-stakes prospect. Give them a smaller, more achievable goal so that you can offer feedback for improvement before taking the training wheels off. Seeing how others can also be successful reinforces the belief in also being able to achieve. Achievability improves performance. This is also important for highly seasoned sales professionals. Seeing short-term success helps people at all levels. We may think that if this person is a "rock star," then they don't need coddling or special considerations.

The reality is that you will need to find out if their "rock star" status is transferrable in your organization. The best place to start is to help them win and win quickly.

A note on the feedback process: Feedback is essential for performance and development. I believe most people understand that feedback is not criticism or, berating or disciplining someone. Rather, it's an information loop that provides a person with what they need to learn and grow. Feedback should be a few things.

Feedback should be neutral. It's not about praise or censure; it's about information. If someone accomplished what you wanted them to, tell them. If they went above and beyond, tell them. If they didn't quite live up to your goal, tell them. It should not be about judgment but rather have a tone of curiosity and interest in what has occurred in order for knowledge to be gathered and change to be implemented. So here are a few ideas on giving negative feedback.

- Ask permission before giving constructive feedback. This can be a simple, "Would you be open to some feedback?" Or perhaps, "Let's go over your most recent performance. When's a good time for you?" Permission is about making sure they're ready and willing to receive the feedback. This is more about timing. If they just lost the deal, you probably want the open wound to heal before pouring salt into it with what will feel like criticism instead of coaching. Openness to feedback will come once the strong emotions are allowed to dissipate a bit.

- If the event was less extreme, you want to give the feedback as close to the occurrence as possible.

- Set expectations and goals. If this is a new role with limited historical context, you may want to break up the goals into manageable components.

- Don't get judgmental. If they failed to close a deal, they failed to close a deal. Look at the actions they took and give them good advice on how to improve. Don't look at the actions they took and make judgments about their character, like, "You lack confidence" or "Your voice is too quiet because you're shy." You don't know the "why" behind their actions, and you don't necessarily have to. **Point them in the direction they need to go and the actions and behaviors that may need modification**.

- Stick to the specific situation you're giving feedback about. This isn't a time to launch into all the faults you've seen from the beginning of your time together. Just deal with one issue at a time and give them space to improve. If all you see are faults, you probably need to get your eyes checked.

- Utilize the Socratic Method of asking questions and letting them come up with a solution themselves. The goal is to help them test their assumptions and gain a deeper understanding of what happened from their vantage point and how that can be rectified or improved. You may also use the 5 Whys approach. If you are not familiar with it, it uses a variation of "Why is that?" or "Why do you think that is the case?" to each answer 5 times.

- Simple and shorter is better. "I'd like to see more of this," and "I'd like to see less of this." Or some variation. You are providing directions without control or emotional baggage attached to it.

Feedback should be useful. It should be regular. Spontaneous is okay, with that permission and openness to receive it at that moment. There's no need to compliment someone's shoes or tell them you disapprove of their haircut (as long as they are adhering to the level of professionalism they agreed to when coming on board). The only feedback you need to provide is the kind that helps them understand how to better succeed at their job.

Feedback should be consistent. It's not necessary to set up a performance review every time your new hire fails or could do better at something. Just make sure to establish a comfortable rapport and **make feedback-sharing the norm** in your organization.

Feedback should be a two-way conversation. Invite questions. Get curious about your new hire. You might uncover ways to help them that aren't process-oriented but rather involve personal development or continuing education. You'll only find out if, over time, you keep the conversation open and continue building a relationship with that person.

Concepts to Revisit

💡 *Brainstorm ways you can help your new sales-person quickly integrate into your team and environment.*

💡 *Make a list of the most important things your new hire needs to learn within the first 90 days. Now, map out a calendar to address each of those elements.*

💡 *Set expectations for goals, development, feedback, performance management, and fol-low-through. Help them understand how they fit into the organization in the long term and strategically.*

Chapter 8:

Retain

*One cannot lead a life that is truly
excellent without feeling that one
belongs to something greater and more
permanent than one self*

- MIHALY CSIKSZENTMIHALYI

*All we can do is influence how they
motivate themselves.*

- RAYMOND WLODKOWSKI

Once you have completed the process of hiring a new salesperson, you come to appreciate the value of retention. Though this chapter is focused on that subject, in truth, everything we've talked about so far plays a role in retention.

There are plenty of other books on the day-to-day management of sales, but it's worthwhile ensuring we address the aspects of the experience that the sales individual will have and why they would be interested in staying in your organization.

Assuming everything throughout the hiring and onboarding processes has gone optimally, you've got a nice foundation. Now, we'll talk about how to approach retention and avoid that nearly 30% turnover rate we talked about in chapter one.

Hierarchy of Needs

While there are many reasons why salespeople either quit or leave for another organization, some of the top ones include dissatisfaction with pay, feeling under-appreciated, poor work-life management, and lack of autonomy. These things get to the heart of the basic human needs and motivations. Abraham Maslow first introduced the concept of an individual's hierarchy of needs in the paper *Theory of Human Motivation* and subsequent books and articles. This theoretical development set the stage for a greater understanding of the complexity of the wants and desires that people gain in the workplace and from the types of work that they do.

To retain talent of any kind, we need to address a couple of key areas of basic individual needs, which include, but aren't limited to:

- Psychological safety

- Meaningful work

- Met economic needs

- Enjoyment of people they work with

Educators have recognized this in children—when a child's physiological or safety needs aren't met, they literally cannot learn what you're trying to teach them. The same thing goes for individuals in any environment – especially the workplace.

Self-actualization
Creativity, problem-solving, authenticity, spontaneity

Esteem
Self-esteem, confidence, achievement

Social needs
Friendship, family

Safety and security

Physiological needs (survival)
Air, shelter, water, food, sleep, sex

While Maslow never explicitly illustrated the needs in a pyramid, human needs do exist, but they can also overlap based on individual preference, type of need, priority, and the environment in which they reside.

With that said, for example, someone can climb to a place of living in abundance in terms of money and love, and if that same person falls (job loss, divorce, etc.), they may find themselves fighting to reclaim their security needs even while focusing on their esteem needs. Abandonment and loss can pull people back to a place of insecurity.

Any new employee will have a collection of needs, wants, and desires. Work can fulfill many aspects of that equation. In the fulfillment of those requirements, an employee can be retained, fulfilled, and contribute to meaningful organizational outcomes. Maslow's hierarchy of needs helps illustrate the layering and interdependence of these aspirations and needs.

As I progress with the rest of this chapter, I will assume that the job meets the basic physiological needs of food, shelter, clothing, etc., that are illustrated in Level 1 of the hierarchy of needs.

Level 2 of the Pyramid: Safety Needs

At this level, compensation is the most impactful. As a smaller organization, this can be a challenge. Your new hire has already agreed to the initial target pay level, but you want to be able to increase their compensation over time. At this point, your success is tied to theirs, and vice versa. The more successful your salesperson, the more revenue you generate, the more you're able to pay your salesperson, and the more empowered they will be to succeed. It's a cycle that requires a small leap of faith both on your part and theirs.

However, if all goes well, over time, reward with increasing levels of compensation when you can, but it is important to recognize the value of other elements of meeting your new hire's safety needs, including transparency, visibility, clarity, fairness, and equity.

Be clear about how to succeed. If your new hire is a self-driven salesperson, one of the few things that can stand in the way of their success is an unclear or poorly defined path to high achievement. Not only will the new hire thrive with a very clearly detailed description of the role responsibility, expectations, and sales process, but they'll also want the positive reinforcement of the incentives clear and visible in the variable pay program. If you've designed everything effectively, your salesperson will meet goals and feel empowered to succeed and continue beyond your expectations.

Offer financial planning services. One great perk for a new hire seeking to fulfill their security needs is optional financial planning counseling or other services. Just like you may have a financial planning service associated with your 401K, you want your sales role to have clarity on how to make money under the plan. Helping your new hires feel financially secure in their personal life will free them up to think more strategically and long-term about their career and desired professional objectives. To be clear, this isn't something that you need to budget and pay for. Many institutions you currently partner with (as a business owner/leader) offer complementary services and educational support for financial services.

Fairness also matters. People tend to be highly tuned to inequities, especially when they are insecure in their sense of belonging to a group or organization. Your new hire may not fit in immediately. And if they feel they are being treated (and paid) unfairly, this will exacerbate their feeling of being an outsider.

Fairness doesn't mean an even distribution of pay but rather an even distribution of opportunity. If you believe you're being fair and your new hire is complaining to you about unfairness, make sure you're communicating well. Be clear and honest with them about any perceived inequities and why they are happening. Perception is reality.

Of course, it may come to be that your new hire sees with fresh eyes something you've missed. So, be open to the possibility that they've spotted an imbalance in the territory allocation, quota sizing, or market opportunity. You will want to address these items with some level of diligence and impartiality.

Level 3 of the Pyramid: Belonging

Belonging means finding your place and how you fit in a job and in the world at large. That's peace in the professional journey. This is psychological security. An organization can fulfill this if it has the trust and openness to allow creativity in work and friendly interaction between peers and supervisors. This can be found with the customer and prospect relationships as well. You want your new salesperson to be comfortable, creative, and take some risks. You don't want them to be fearful to try something new to gain the attention of prospects or gain loyalty from customers. Boldness and confidence come in an environment such as this.

Team building is an essential part of the relationship development experience for any new hire. It's important that they meet and connect with everyone on the team. Components that belong in a team environment are mutual respect, good conflict resolution skills, a positive outlook, and maybe a splash of fun (hopefully, that's a part of your culture!).

As they get focused on executing against their sales objectives quickly, the sales employee may be so externally focused that they aren't giving attention to their internal stakeholder team that can assist them in being successful in their professional journey (sales needs support inside and outside of the org). Your leadership can help shed light on that potential gap in the belonging equation.

Defining their place in the organizational plan also helps fulfill the "respect and belonging" need. Salespeople are likely to be largely motivated by individual goals, but giving them a sense of what they are accomplishing in the larger organization helps create engagement, connection, and purpose in their work. It also helps reduce some of the strife that seems to crop up between the sales team and the operations team.[24]

Level 4 of the Pyramid: Esteem

Esteem is the aspiration to get to a point of meaningful work and fulfillment through progression. At this level, extrinsic rewards, such as bonuses or personal praise, are primarily symbolic. A pay raise is an acknowledgment of work done above and beyond. A plaque is a symbol of a special achievement. The real reward is achievement and the confidence that comes from growth and development. Mastery in the profession of persuasion and influence is the reward unto itself. Recognize that at this level, much of the emphasis shifts internally.

Note: This isn't to say that extrinsic rewards no longer matter. Work (and its financial rewards) may have shifted attention to aspects beyond immediate security needs with new areas like grandchildren, charities, or that trip of a lifetime.

Feedback should be consistent. Whether you have positive things to say or constructive criticism, make sure you are providing feedback and coaching on a regular basis. There is greater personal value and appreciation of this guidance at this level.

Challenges and stretch goals can build esteem. If your new hire is crushing their goals and looking for more, you can help them grow both professionally and personally by raising the bar. Determine what opportunities exist beyond the quota target to give your new hire something bigger to reach for. That may be leadership functions they want to start to explore.

Career development should be offered. The opportunity for career advancement is an oft-cited factor in retention. If your new hire doesn't reach out to you, be sure to remind them that they are more than welcome to schedule time to discuss their future with your organization. But it can be of greater value to ask so they know you are thinking about it.

Questions they may have in a career development conversation may include:

- What's next after this?

- What's next for me here?

- How can I prepare for a promotion to the next level of my career?

- I'm interested in leadership positions. Where do I start?

- Do you offer educational assistance for advanced degrees or certifications?

- How can I continue to hone my craft?

- What do I need to do to keep getting better at what I do?

Your goal should be to provide them with clear, honest information so that they can make the right choices for their career progression. And if you're worried that your organization may not be able to offer an attractive enough future, just remember that when push comes to shove, individuals will prefer security, comfort, and job clarity over the unpredictable.

Level 5 of the Pyramid: Self-actualization

Self-actualization is the final stage in the hierarchy of needs. In their professional life, this means they've found work that makes them feel fulfilled and allows them to stretch their talents and become their best selves. At this stage, the rewards of work are more fully intrinsic, i.e., happening inside themselves. They appreciate the work for the sake of the work and find reward in understanding and aligning with meaning and values.

This is when we are beyond the money as a 'motivation' conversation because they know what they like, what they want to get out of the work, and how they can realize it professionally. This awareness of personal strengths and weaknesses can be honed for optimal organizational outcomes.

The mindset shifts – recognizing fulfillment comes from within. They understand that the money will come as long as they are able to continue the work that they enjoy, and it provides fulfillment at a much deeper level. This is when they transition from chasing the money to having the money chase them (so to speak).

At this point, your sales employee may be content to continue to refine their skill set in selling, or they may desire to grow further into mentorship or a leadership position. If you notice they're looking for ways to contribute to the organization beyond sales, consider their potential for advancement.

A Note on Motivation

Rewards look different depending on the makeup of your needs. There are two types of motivation and two types of rewards — intrinsic and extrinsic. Intrinsic rewards are the internal gratifications you get when you achieve your own goals. You may finish a woodworking project and feel exhilarated and proud even though there's no one around to appreciate the moment, praise you, or reward you. These can be felt in the celebration of aspects of personal autonomy, creativity, or the mastery of a task. That's an intrinsic reward—fulfillment in the act of doing the work without any external control or validation.

Extrinsic rewards come from the outside. Your boss gives you a pay raise, you're nominated for an award, or your child tells you you're the best parent in the world. These are extrinsic rewards.

It's good to get to know your new hire and where they are in their career journey. If they're just getting established and that paycheck matters a lot more to them, they'll likely be more motivated by extrinsic rewards like bonuses and pay raises. If they're in a good place financially and now focused on taking ownership of their career, they'll more likely be motivated by the intrinsic rewards that come with challenges, opportunities, and progression of their skills.

Retention

As your organization grows, you'll be able to retain happy, productive, upwardly mobile employees.

Put the work into maintaining a needs-fulfilling retention strategy, and you'll reap rewards for years to come. Retention of talent is about setting individuals up for success in their present and future roles. It requires providing a vision of a future with the organization as well as clarity of the responsibilities and expectations of the function. It also requires transparency of how pay works, acknowledgment and recognition of performance, and creating an environment that is psychologically safe, collaborative, and purposeful. By adding meaning and value to the work being done and simultaneously producing ever-expanding business and professional outcomes for both parties to share, you've found the special sauce.

As it relates to the retention of sales employees more specifically, much of the effort should go into providing sufficient incentives and a path for overachievement and establishing a quality environment where that is possible – one in which they can climb that mountain of needs and deliver ever-increasing business results that can be celebrated by the organization.

Concepts to Revisit

💡 *Do a needs assessment to see where the new salesperson currently resides in the hierarchy of needs upon entry into the organization.*

💡 *If their current position differs greatly from their aspiration, then you will want to offer a bridge to help support them on that journey to higher-level needs. Provide a narrative and vision of the future with them in the organization. Share that vision and allow for open commentary to see how they are aligned (or differ). Evaluate for fit and identify steps for development.*

💡 *The new employee isn't showing up as a blank slate. They are coming to the organization with some aspects of security, safety, aspiration, etc., in tow. The best thing you can do is see if what you can offer is congruent with their needs. Define what level of time and financial investment you are willing to offer for all of your employees on their path of growth.*

Chapter 9:
A Word on Agencies

Everybody has a plan until they get punched in the face

- MIKE TYSON

Your employees are your company's real competitive advantage. They're the ones making the magic happen – so long as their needs are being met.

- RICHARD BRANSON

R ecruitment agencies can be a valuable resource, but there are some points of caution to take into consideration. In this chapter, I won't make a recommendation one way or the other, but rather, I will cover the pros and cons of using an agency and how you can have a positive experience if you choose to go the agency route.

Agency Pros

Agencies already have a talent pipeline. In chapter four, we talked about creating a talent pipeline. This takes time and attention. It's extremely valuable as your organization grows, but if you don't have the time or capacity to maintain relationships with potential future candidates, agencies can be of great benefit.

A good agency—especially one that specializes in your organization's niche or sector—will keep a healthy, growing pipeline of talent prospects. They'll nurture this list by regularly getting updates so that they aren't wasting your time inviting applicants who are no longer available.

Agencies can fill your role faster. Assuming you've read the first eight chapters of this book, or if you've ever hired before, you know what a time-consuming process it is. Not only can an agency free up your time, but it can also get the job done faster. Thanks to their existing talent pipeline as well as their well-oiled screening process, you'll likely see a prospective employee much faster if you don't go it alone.

Agencies have insights that can help you. As an employer, you're only hiring for your organization on an as-needed basis. Agencies are hiring for multiple organizations all the time. Because of this, they have data and insights on hiring trends that can help them make more efficient decisions than a private employer. Agencies are less likely to mismatch talent with your role. They may send you fewer candidates than you would get on your own, but those candidates are qualified through their screening process.

Agency Cons

Agencies come with fees. This is an obvious one, but you have to find that balance between convenience and cost. Which can you afford? Sometimes, you have to pay in time rather than money, so if agency fees are going to put you further into the red than you can afford right now, it may be best to go it alone for now.

Agencies lack insight into your culture. Agencies are great at matching you with a candidate based on job qualifications and role responsibilities, but they aren't great at finding good cultural fits. Because you are just one of many clients an agency is hiring for; they're not as likely to take the time to get to know a candidate's values and goals as you would be if you did the hiring yourself. Only you can really drive the values, mission, and purpose home.

Agencies aren't as concerned with your company's brand and reputation. Building your brand identity isn't just a marketing process. Hiring is also an opportunity to put your best foot forward, build your brand, and establish quality connections. Your reputation is on the line as well while you begin the process of building these new relationships. Reputation is also critical when you put that salesperson in front of your customers. No one knows your organization like you.

Agencies don't have as much at stake. They have their processes and don't have time to white-label their service with your brand message (unless you do a lot of business with them). Generally, they're just going to be focused on filling the position. They will be less likely to consider alignment of reputation in the hiring process.

💡 Make a list of the things that are important to you in a candidate. Now, identify which of those things fall under the category of values, culture, skill, or experience. If you sorted this based on priority, which can be translated effectively by an agency?

How to Work With An Agency

If the cost isn't a factor for you, and you're leaning towards going with an agency, you want to think about this with a long-term lens. It's a good idea to interview the agency and their representatives as though you are preparing for a long-term partnership. It's important to make sure you're not just one of hundreds of nameless accounts. Their recruiter will be able to represent your organization better if you've built a solid relationship. Here are some tips to help you get the most out of working with a recruiting agency.

Build a partnership with your agency. Establish ongoing communications with your agency so that you can help them evolve their efforts to meet your expectations. Ultimately, you want to grow in rapport over time and gain a trusted ally to connect you with the best possible talent whenever you need it. Your agency should be more than a vendor; it should be a business partnership.

Find a staffing agency that specializes in your niche. Salespeople come in all forms, and their abilities can be related to what they're selling—especially if they've only worked in one industry. A large-scale staffing agency may not be taking time to differentiate qualifications based on your specialized industry. Before engaging an agency, do some pre-screening to make sure they are at least familiar with your niche or, better yet, that they specialize in it.

Interview agencies to see what kind of service you'll be getting. An agency can be a partner for decades, so it's a good idea to start off on the right foot. Spend some time interviewing to find out not only their technical qualifications but also if you feel a good rapport with them. If they share similar values and understand your company culture, they can better filter candidates not only on qualifications but also on cultural fit.

Be specific about your needs. When you're describing a role, make sure to be as specific as possible, including all the information and details you've gathered when framing up the role. Use language like "more of this experience" or "less of that type of work" to give them a range of fit (and resumé language) when looking for a candidate.

Make sure you're absolutely ready to fill the role and respond in a timely manner. Besides wasting your time and theirs, engaging an agency when you're not fully committed to hiring is a bad way to start a relationship. Agencies have their own reputations to look out for, so if the talent they're sending your way isn't hearing back from you, that's going to look bad on the agency. If you are questioning your decision to hire, take some more time to get very clear on whether it's the right time. You can go back to Chapter 1 of this book for tips on determining whether to hire now or not.

Keep in contact after the hire. No one likes a friend who only calls when they need something. You don't have to email every day, but it's a good idea to stay in touch with your contact at your recruiting agency. You can do this through LinkedIn or by dropping them an occasional email. Let them know how you're doing with the new hire and see if they have any market insights to share. Chances are, you'll need to hire again, and maintaining contact will help grow the relationship in the in-between times.

💡 Make your own pros and cons list for whether an agency works for you or not. Only you can decide what's best right now for you and your organization.

Which Way is Best?

It's okay to use an agency. It's okay not to use an agency. It's all down to what works best for you. Chances are good if you're on either end of the spectrum—either a small organization or a very large one—you're going to do your hiring in-house. As a small organization, you may not be able to afford an agency. And if you grow big enough to handle it in-house, you're going to want to manage your own talent pipeline so you can better control your brand identity and keep an eye on your prospective employees.

However, if you do choose to go the agency route, invest in the partnership up-front, doing the work of researching and interviewing to make sure you've at least got the potential for a long-term partnership.

Conclusion

High achievement always takes place in the framework of high expectation.

- Charles Kettering

Perfection is not attainable. But if we chase perfection, we can catch excellence.

- Vince Lombardi

This book is intended to serve as a practical guide for those less familiar with the process of bringing on sales talent. Since sales is the lifeblood of every organization, this is a clear and beneficial resource for organizations of every size and individuals from every leadership level.

The book started with a prompt to get creative and truly understand whether your organization was ready for that new sales position. That naturally extended into clarifying the role and investing time in defining expectations of the function, explicitly documenting the coverage model and commercial strategy, and demonstrating the path to success. Sales activities were identified and linked to organizational outcomes, and those aspects of work in the sales process were outlined to help summarize the job (and, ultimately, the right candidate). This pre-work on job content was recognized as crucial to the clarity of the role and responsibilities while also being critical for the long-term success of the salesperson in the position.

Chapter 3 covered compensation. While that isn't the primary focus of the book, we covered the core elements needed to attract, retain, and motivate any individual at work. This section illustrated the need for organizations to spend time developing the underlying compensation philosophy - intentionally defining what it values, why it values it, and what type of work gets rewarded. The chapter finishes with a tactical guide when your company can't compete with market levels or if the budget isn't available for the job level initially desired.

The next section entails the hiring process, starting with attracting and marketing of the job – how and where. It is helpful to ensure you have some level of an employee value proposition in place to have effective talking points for your recruiting process.

It is important to recognize that your process for interviewing and screening candidates follows a process – clear and defined – so as to remove bias and increase the speed of the experience for all parties involved.

Once you reach the point of deciding on who you want to hire, the work isn't over. There are candidates to decline, and you may want to do that without losing them as potential candidates for future roles. There's also the phrasing of the actual offer, the presentation, and the negotiation.

In Chapter 7, we move on to the environment after the new salesperson has been for the job. Your first 90 days are crucial to the success and longevity of your new employee, but keep in mind that it can take up to a full 12 months to have any new salesperson fully ramped up.

After hiring, you're playing a long game, making sure to lay the groundwork for retention. It pays to consider your employees' needs in balance with the needs of the organization.

Finally, the book comes to a close with a few words on utilizing agencies. There are, of course, pros and cons to using an agency for your hiring process, and only you can determine what's best for your organization.

The sales team is crucial to the health of your organization. They are the drivers of growth and revenue, so it seems appropriate to think about how best to support their growth as well.

An intentional plan of action for hiring not only helps you identify the right fit for your role but also sets up the possibility for a long-term relationship that is mutually beneficial. If the partnership isn't working for both parties, action will have to be taken—whether that's amending any conflicts or parting ways—otherwise, both the employee and organization will suffer.

Keep in mind that this book offers a lot of tactical best practices, which may not all apply to your specific organization. The main takeaway is the advocacy that both sides understand their needs and values as early as possible in the process of hiring so that they will each experience better outcomes and alignment for long-term success.

It is my hope that you can successfully connect your vision with the right people to accomplish many amazing things together. You will both be greater because of it.

Thanks,
Christopher

Appendix A:
Favorite Interview Questions

I recently asked several associates in sales what their favorite interview questions were when hiring for sales. Below is a compilation of their answers.

Getting to Know You Questions:

1. What is your story? How did you arrive here for this interview?

   - Gives your candidate a chance to loosen up. During this question, you can evaluate how well they perform under pressure as well as their storytelling ability.

2. What accomplishments are you most proud of and why? (Personal and Professional)

- This is a good opportunity to see what they value in their lives.

3. What was your greatest setback/failure, and what did you learn from it?

4. In your opinion, what are the (3) most important qualities of being an effective leader?

5. What makes you successful?

6. What would your peers say about you?

- *Trying to get a sense of self-awareness.*

7. In your view, how did the pandemic change the sales environment and sales process? What are the keys to adapting to the new post-pandemic era?

8. How do you prioritize your time and ensure you're spending it on the highest-priority activities that will drive results?

Teamwork Questions:

1. Give me an example of how you needed to build consensus to achieve a goal.

2. Can you discuss a time when you had to work cross-functionally within an organization to

achieve a business goal? What was your role, and how did you ensure everyone was on the same page?

Situational Sales Interview Questions:

1. How would you approach a short sales cycle differently than a long sales cycle?

   - Short cycles call for reps that can close quickly, and long sales cycles require a much more careful, tailored approach. They're drastically different, and your candidate should recognize this.

2. When do you stop pursuing a client?

   - The right answer here will depend on your company's process, but in general, the more tenacious and persistent a rep is willing to be, the better. Trish Bertuzzi, the founder of The Bridge Group, recommends six to eight attempts before throwing in the towel.

3. How do you keep a smile on your face during a hard day?

   - Appraise the person's attitude towards rejection. Do they need time to shake off an unpleasant conversation? Or do they bounce back immediately? See which strategies they use to recover and move on.

4. Have you ever turned a prospect away? If so, why?

   • Selling to everyone and anyone — even if a salesperson knows it's not in the prospect's best interest — is a recipe for disaster. Make sure your candidate is comfortable with turning business away if the potential customer isn't a good fit.

5. What experience do you have in complex and consultative sales, and what are your key strengths in this area?

6. How do you research potential clients and identify new business opportunities? Can you walk me through your process?

7. How do you typically approach a new business prospect or lead? Can you give an example of a successful approach you've used in the past?

8. How do you manage a sales pipeline and prioritize leads and opportunities?

9. How do you stay up to date on industry trends and changes that might impact your sales strategies?

10. Have you ever had to negotiate a complex deal with a client or partner? Can you give an example of the negotiation process and outcome?

Technical Sales Interview Questions:

1. How do you keep up to date on your target market?

   - Even if the target market of their last job is totally different from the one they're interviewing for, this will show their ability to find and keep up with relevant trade publications and blogs. Dig deeper and ask for a recent piece of information they've learned from one of the publications.

2. In your last position, how much time did you spend cultivating customer relationships versus hunting for new clients, and why?

   - Certain companies and roles call for people who are better at farming or hunting, but look out for a person who performs one of these tasks to the exclusion of the other. Both are vital to sales.

3. What are your favorite questions to ask prospects?

- Good salespeople spend more time asking questions than pitching. Look out for open-ended questions that will help a rep thoroughly understand a prospect's needs.

4. What's your approach to handling customer objections?

- Preparing to deal with objections — instead of winging it — is critical. Listen for evidence of a process.

Inside Sales Interview Questions:

1. Explain the steps you take from the beginning of the sales process to the end.

- This shows how well your candidate understands and considers the sales process. It also illustrates how they organize their thoughts and communicate complicated concepts.

- Do they explain their process clearly? And do they cover the main steps: prospect, connect, research/evaluate, present, and close? These are two things you should look for in their answer.

2. Tell me about an objection you had trouble overcoming over the phone. How did you finally move the deal forward?

- Every salesperson has at least one objection that plagues them. Did the candidate listen to the prospect's concerns, validate their concerns, and help them reach a different conclusion?

- The answer to this question will tell you a lot about how your candidate solves problems and thinks strategically.

3. Walk me through the most successful steps you took to land your most successful sale.

- This question aims to better understand the candidate's thought process as they approach a sale. Additionally, it is a good way to showcase their strengths using a real-life example.

4. Tell me about a time you didn't close a deal. What did you learn from that experience?

- Everyone loses deals, and it's ok to talk about it. This question aims to dive into the lessons the candidate has learned and how they have improved their sales techniques from less-than-stellar deals.

Fit and Motivation Sales Interview Questions:

1. What's worse: Not making quota every single month or not having happy customers?

   - Depending on your company's goals, either answer could be the right one. But beware of reps who will prioritize quota over truly giving customers what they need — or withholding what they don't.

2. What's your least favorite part of the sales process?

   - If their least favorite part is the most important part at your company, that's probably a red flag. Ask them what they do to simplify their least favorite part of the process or make it more enjoyable. This question can also alert you to weak areas.

3. What motivates you?

- Money, achievement, helping customers, being #1 — there are a lot of potential answers to this question. What makes a good answer versus a bad one will hinge on your company culture. For instance, if teamwork is an important aspect of your sales team, a candidate who is driven by internal competition might not be a great fit.

4. What's your take on collaboration within a sales team?

- Collaboration might be less important at some organizations than others, but candidates who aren't willing to collaborate at all likely won't make pleasant coworkers. Their uncooperative attitude will also block knowledge sharing.

5. Who are you most comfortable selling to and why?

- Listen for whether they answer with a description of an ideal buyer, or a demographic with no tie-in to the buying process. Depending on your product or service, the second type of response might pose a problem.

6. What's your opinion of the role of learning in sales?

- Being thrown for a loop by this question is a sign your candidate isn't a life-long learner — an increasingly important trait in salespeople. An ideal candidate should communicate they're willing to learn and grow in their role.

7. How would you describe the culture at your last company?

- This tells you a lot about what the candidate values, how they work with others, and what kind of leadership they thrive under. If they complain about long hours or rigid goals and your company thrives off the energy created by late nights and challenging numbers, it's probably not the right fit.

8. Describe your ideal sales manager.

- Asking a candidate to describe their ideal manager shows you how autonomous they are, how they approach working relationships, and how they overcome challenges. Look for a candidate who's able to work independently and is comfortable taking direction from their boss.

9. Other than hitting your numbers, what other intrinsic value can you provide to the organization?

- This is another question that gets to the heart of culture and fit.

10. Are you a scientist who can sell or a salesperson who loves science? What is better and why?

- Note that there is no wrong answer here. I am just trying to get a sense of what their approach is.

- And this question can easily be adapted to any area of technical or value-based selling in your industry.

Appendix B:
Hiring for Sales Checklist

Before You Hire

- ☐ Think about your next organizational target. Are you looking to scale, or will you be satisfied with growth?

- ☐ Is there any other way you can achieve your goals besides hiring a new salesperson?

- ☐ What is your capacity? Are you maxed out with the resources you have? Could you do more?

- ☐ Compare a projection of your capabilities for penetrating the market by yourself against your capabilities with a new hire.

☐ Keep in mind that sales rep turnover is more than double the average turnover rate of other roles, and the average tenure is 18 months—are you prepared to experience that?

Defining the role

☐ Write down the behaviors that you want to see in your salesperson's interactions with coworkers and customers.

☐ Write down the behaviors you don't want to see. This will help you interview with clarity later on and not compromise any "gut" feelings you might have about subtle behavioral cues.

☐ In startups and smaller organizations, salespeople often have to fulfill multiple roles. Even if this is the case, map out your sales pipeline. Look at where the burden of sales falls now. Rather than trying to hire for the entire sales process, pick the point on the map where a sales representative can create the biggest impact.

☐ Once you've gathered market data and analyzed the pay ranges in your own company, go ahead and try your hand at writing a job description. Resist the urge to copy from Indeed or LinkedIn and write your description from scratch. Don't be afraid to infuse some personality into it— this will give your prospective hire a feel for the tone and culture of your workplace.

Competitive Assessment

☐ Write your compensation philosophy.

☐ Make a list of compensable factors in your job description.

☐ What education and experience levels are you looking for?

  o What are the working conditions your new hire will be expected to perform in?

  o How much or how little supervision do you intend to give them?

☐ Go find jobs that fit what you are trying to accomplish. Pick five job descriptions ranging from the low end to the high end of the market pay spectrum. List out each salary, pay mix (if specified), and compensable factors.

☐ Does anything need to change about your job description? If so, now is the time to do it. Go ahead and complete any modifications before posting. You don't want to get caught in any conflicting messaging or expectations.

Attracting Talent

☐ Review your company values and really think about what you want for your new employee before writing out your Employee Value Proposition.

Screening

☐ Thinking about how to show important information about your prospective hire, craft some interview questions that will show whether this person has the behaviors you're looking for in a candidate.

☐ Write your pre-screening phone call script.

☐ Document your process so you can manage to it. It should include interview questions, timing expectations, process and number of interviews, FAQs, description of the role, and scripts if you need to rely on them.

☐ Ask about pay challenges, objectives, or issues that need to be overcome based on what they know.

☐ You've already spoken about compensation. Be sure you cover that early on.

Making the Offer

☐ Using the information you've gathered so far, craft an offer letter to your ideal candidate. Don't forget to factor in market value and internal equity when deciding on final offers.

☐ If you don't already subscribe to an app or system for digital documents, retention, and signatures, do some research. The right program can help you track and maintain your contracts with automation. This is just a small way you can increase efficiency at a low cost.

Onboarding

☐ Brainstorm ways you can help your new hire more easily integrate into your team and environment.

☐ Make a list of the most important things your new hire needs to learn within the first 90 days. Now, map out a calendar to address each of those elements.

☐ Set expectations for goals, development, feedback, performance management, and follow-through. Help them understand how they fit into the organization long term.

Retain

☐ The new salesperson isn't showing up as a blank slate. They are coming to the organization with some aspects of security, safety, aspiration, etc., in tow. The best thing you can do is see if what you can offer is congruent with their needs. Take the time to define what level of investment you are willing to offer for your employees on their path of growth.

Agencies

☐ Make a list of the things that are important to you in a candidate. Now, identify which of those things fall under the category of values, culture, skill, or experience. If you sorted this based on priority, which can be translated effectively by an agency?

☐ Make your own pros and cons list for whether an agency works for you or not. Only you can decide what's best right now for you and your organization.

Get your copy of the Checklist here:

Acknowledgments

*The two most important warriors
are patience and time.*

- LEO TOLSTOY

It has been an amazing few years to watch and experience. Lots of changes and shifts in the labor market. And they have gone both ways. High labor supply, high labor demand. Shortages. Employee retention. Large swings in wage changes and then unemployment. During that time, the number one need in any organization is revenue and the need for quality sales talent.

This book continues my adventure of writing and developing expertise in sales operations and compensation, and I have a group of people who have been extremely supportive and integral to my successes. The list includes Abby Letner, who serves as my editor, copywriter, and sounding board for creative writing thoughts and tangents. Tonya Fuschetti, who developed the cover art and overall design of the branding. Rich Marra has been my long-time mentor and advisor in my professional development. Thank you all!!

I'd also like to thank advanced readers and contributors for their commentary and guidance as they provided commentary to improve the content between the covers of this book. I want to personally thank Karen Heier, Christine Rieser, Urvashi Gupta, Bill Keyes, Kate Palazzolo, Ali Ghiassi, Rich Marra, and Brad Leggett.

Also, special thanks to Catherine Canales, Jim Shircliff, Ali Ghiassi, Shannon Fox, Urvashi Gupta, Karen Heier, Annette Helberg, Peter Davison, Dario Campos, Judy Rubin, and Bryan Harley for sharing some of their favorite sales interview questions that fill the pages of this appendix.

For all of those not mentioned who have been inspirational in the advancement of this content and my personal and professional development, I am forever eternally grateful.

Lastly, thank you to all of the employees and employers of salespeople, as you make this world go round!

Please do reach out to me directly at christopher@salescompguy.com if you have any questions or comments about the contents of this book. Thanks again for your support!

About the Author

Christopher Goff has over 18 years of experience in the areas of Compensation and Sales Operations. He frequently speaks to organizations on the best practices of pay programs across the spectrum of rewards.

Christopher holds an MBA from Rasmussen University, a Master's degree in Economics from North Carolina State University, and a Bachelor of Science degree in Finance from Catawba College. Christopher is a Certified Compensation Professional (CCP), a Global Remuneration Professional (GRP), and a Certified Sales Compensation Professional (CSCP) through WorldatWork.

Christopher serves on the Faculty of WorldatWork and is an Adjunct at Catawba

College. You can also find many of Christopher's musings on LinkedIn as well as https://www.salescompguy.com/blog.

He is the author of multiple books on the subjects of pay transparency and sales compensation. His many books can be found here: https://www.amazon.com/stores/Christopher-Goff/author/B09ZGWJMYP

Starting Simple: Sales Compensation

STARTING SIMPLE:
Sales Compensation

BY CHRISTOPHER GOFF

Every organization reaches a crossroads— either grow or die. How are you preparing your organization for growth and, more importantly, sustainability? What actions are you taking to ensure your organization is prepared for the aggressive labor market and high demand for sales talent today?

This book is intended for startups and non-profits alike that are looking for growth through sales. As you embark on the surprisingly complex path to hiring your first salesperson, this book will give you clear guidance on how to effectively attract, motivate, and retain sales-persons with an effective compensation plan.

You'll learn:

- The principles of successful sales compensation practices

- Practical and easy-to-understand guidance for hiring your first salesperson

- Step-by-step processes for establishing a sales incentive plan from scratch

- Foundational steps for implanting an incentive strategy that will grow along with your company

While guidance provided within these pages is focused on small organizations, the basic principles can easily be applied to an organization of any size that is launching a new product, entering a new geography or market segment, or building out a brand-new division. Each and every step of growth requires a revisit to the basics of sales compensation in order for your organization to stay relevant and competitive.

Diving headlong into the hiring process without first addressing the issues outlined in this book can result in damage to your company culture, your employee morale, and your bottom line. Take the time to follow these steps, and you'll have laid the groundwork for sustainable growth through sales in your organization.

Shop Now
Starting Simple: Pay Transparency

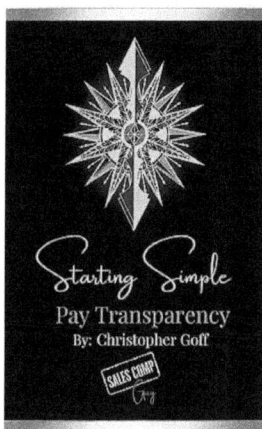

The times—and laws—are changing. *Starting Simple: Pay Transparency* is both a warning message and a guide for organizations facing sudden and dramatic legal requirements for how they manage compensation.

Writing in response to California's comprehensive pay transparency law, 16-year veteran compensation and sales operations comp advisor, Christopher Goff, guides you through the process of preparing your organization for pay transparency. Inside you'll find:

- Information on two of the most disruptive and demanding pay transparency laws in the United States

- How to collect the data you'll need to meet compliance for reporting

- Instructions on how to build out your pay structures

- Guidance on how to analyze your data for disparities

- A FREE downloadable checklist to get you from start to finish so that you're ready if and when your state increases its reporting requirements

This guide in no way constitutes legal guidance. Instead, it offers practical strategies for organizing your pay structure in a way that makes it easier for you to adapt to changes in pay transparency and reporting laws.

Shop Now
Starting Simple: Finding Fairness

Starting Simple: Finding Fairness

By Chistopher Goff

Pay transparency laws are sweeping the nation and bringing new awareness to the ideas of fairness and equity in the workplace. But establishing fairness in base pay is a reasonably straightforward—if labor-intensive—process. The real challenges come in providing the experience of fairness for your employees when a large portion of the pay is based on performance.

Starting Simple: Finding Fairness is designed for executives, human resources leaders, and sales managers who are looking for solid guidance on the process of institutionalizing fairness for their sales population.

In this book, you'll find:

- Definitions of fairness, equality, and equity as they relate to a sales compensation program

- Direction on how to build a sales culture built foundationally on fairness, with the help of a step-by-step checklist

- Explanations of how bias can influence how you hire, pay, and promote

- Strategies for identifying sources of inequities that need to be addressed

- Guidance on creating an equitable distribution of opportunity, setting quotas, and assigning territories

Although there are plenty of examples and guidelines, ultimately, this book is designed to illuminate all the points of vulnerability that can exist within a variable pay program, as well as offer tips on how to approach and strengthen each of these points.

Shop Now

Notes

1   Boskamp, Elsie. 2023. *Zippia: The Career Expert.* February 16. https://www.zippia.com/advice/cost-of-hiring-statistics-average-cost-per-hire/#Recruitment_Statistics

2   HBR. 2017. "How to Predict Turnover On Your Sales Team." *Harvard Business Review*, July-August: 22-24.

3   Bureau of Labor Statistics, https://www.bls.gov/oes/2023/may/oes_nat.htm#41-0000

4   Horstman, Mark. (2020). *The Effective Hiring Manager* (p. 5). Wiley.

5   LinkedIn. 2017. "Global Recruiting Trends 2017."

6   Bidwell, Matthew. n.d. *Paying More to Get Less: The Effects of External Hiring Versus Internal Mobility.* 2012: University of Pennsylvania.

7   The Bridge Group. n.d. "Sales Development Metrics and Comp Report."

8   Rigoni, Brandon, and Jim Asplund. 2016. *Global Study: ROI for Strengths-Based Development.* September 22.

9   Tayan, Brian. 2019. *The Wells Fargo Cross-Selling Scandal.* Stanford, February.

10 Cichelli, David J. 2020. *Compensating the Sales Force: A Practical Guide to Designing Winning Sales Reward Programs, Third Edition.* McGraw Hill.

11 (Horstman, The Effective Hiring Manager 2020)

12 Cichelli, David J. 2020. *Compensating the Sales Force: A Practical Guide to Designing Winning Sales Reward Programs, Third Edition*. McGraw Hill.; 47.

13 Carroll, Stacey. 2009. *What is a Compensation Philosophy? How to Write One*. September 15th

14 Hampton. 2022. *A Guide to Designing a Compensation Philosophy*. December 23.

15 n.d. *Nike Careers*. Accessed October 2024. https://jobs.nike.com/.

16 n.d. *Apple Careers*. Accessed October 2024. https://www.apple.com/careers/us/

17 n.d. *Harver Careers*. Accessed October 2024. https://harver.com/careers/

18 LinkedIn. n.d. *4 Ways to Hire Fast on a Budget*.

19 (Horstman, The Effective Hiring Manager 2020); 31.

20 Glassdoor Team. 2021. *How to Keep Second Place Candidates Interested*. July 22.

21 Gallup. n.d. "Create an Exceptional Onboarding Journey for Your New Employees."

22 Ibid.

23 Federal Trade Commission. 2024. *FTC Announces Rule Banning Noncompetes*. April 23.

24 Schoenbeck, Dave. 2017. *The Age Old Business Battle: Sales vs. Operations*. September 21.